BLITZ KIDS

BLITZ KIDS

THE CINDERELLA STORY OF THE 1944 UNIVERSITY OF UTAH NATIONAL CHAMPIONSHIP BASKETBALL TEAM

Josh Ferrin and Tres Ferrin

GIBBS SMITH
TO ENRICH AND INSPIRE HUMANKIND

This book is for Seth, whose life taught us to live
passionately, to never look away from a challenge,
and that not knowing how to do something
shouldn't prevent you from doing it.

First Edition
16 15 14 13 12   5 4 3 2 1

Text © 2012 Josh Ferrin and Tres Ferrin

Published by
Gibbs Smith
P.O. Box 667
Layton, Utah 84041

1.800.835.4993 orders
www.gibbs-smith.com

Designed by Kurt Wahlner
Printed and bound in the United States

Gibbs Smith books are printed on either recycled, 100% post-consumer
waste, FSC-certified papers or on paper produced from sustainable PEFC-
certified forest/controlled wood source. Learn more at www.pefc.org.

Library of Congress Cataloging-in-Publication Data

Ferrin, Josh.
  Blitz kids : the cinderella story of the 1944 University of Utah national
championship basketball team / Josh Ferrin and Tres Ferrin. — 1st ed.
      p. cm.
  Includes index.
  ISBN 978-1-4236-2494-3
1. Runnin' Utes (Basketball team)—History. 2. University of
Utah—Basketball—History. I. Ferrin, Tres. II. Title.
  GV885.43.U583F47 2012
  796.323'6309792258—dc23
                              2011038363

CONTENTS

FOREWORD

I sympathize with Eeyore. Wherever he goes a dark cloud follows, drizzling rain on his dismal head. He can't escape it, and it has made him who he is. My specter is not bleak or dark, nor does it pour despair down on me. In fact, it inspires me in all I do. But it is there with me always.

It is my history.

My father was the one in the family who had a passion for telling stories, most of which were cunningly designed to scare the willies out of his children. He crafted stories of old Indian chiefs who haunted the lake and would snatch unfortunate little children out of the morning mist if they were unwise enough to venture out into the water alone. His face would sharpen with glee as he spun his tale of "The Monkey's Paw" or "The Black Pumpkin."

Yet, the stories that would fill me with the most delight were not the scary ones, not the ones that would frighten the babysitter, nor the made-up yarns about specters or spirits. The amazing tales that filled me with intrigue were true and have stayed with me. They were the stories of how the soft-spoken giant I called Grandpa Arnie, along with an equally uncanny group of cadres, had defied the game of basketball and become champions. To a child of the 1980s, my grandpa was Rocky. But instead of boxing, he played basketball.

Not many remember what happened and how my grandpa was part of what is perhaps the greatest underdog story in the history of college basketball. To the rest of the world, this story is known but has never been told in its entirety. It is a tragedy in the truest sense. It is a tale of the greatest achievements but also a story of death and loss.

There is a very simple reason I want to tell this story and share it with others: it is because I am a father of two young boys. As I look at all the idols of our society today and the variety of influences that will come into their lives, I want them to know of their history and the stories that inspire me, stories that teach that they can accomplish anything, no matter the odds against them.

Eeyore and I both have constant companions. His are doubt and fear. Mine, on the other hand, is a history that I bear with honor. That history has made me who I am and inspires me to strive for excellence and goodness.

As today's basketball fans, we often become caught up in the bravado of the dunk and the attitude of the trash-talker. We wear clothing that bears the names of our sports heroes, and if those heroes wear jewelry, we wear jewelry. To show our devotion, we wear our favorite team's logo tattooed on our skin. For many of us, the game of basketball has become more than a sport; it has become an important part of our culture and part of who we are.

There was a time when the game of college basketball was not big business; a time before HDTV and bidding wars for broadcast rights. It was a time when families would gather together around a radio in the living room and listen to fast-talking sports broadcasters paint verbal portraits of the action on the court. In the early 1940s, basketball was played for the passion of the competition, not for large professional contracts and multimillion-dollar shoe deals. People were fans because it was a pure sport void of all the hype, an additive it didn't need.

This is a story of athletes who helped to establish the roots of the game of basketball. Because of the dedication and hard work of these early pioneers, the fledgling NCAA Tournament of the '40s caught the public's interest and has evolved to become the greatest event in all of sport. These athletes were pioneers before the giants came. They played the game for one reason and one reason alone: they loved it.

—Josh Ferrin

INTRODUCTION

It must have been magic. Whatever possessed them had transformed these unknown kids from a far-away place into something greater than themselves. It was as if by some ancient alchemy gold had been extracted from the salty Utah earth. They were a ragtag team of kids wearing borrowed shoes and loaner jockstraps—giants in boys' frames, elevated beyond their humble beginnings to the status of kings who ruled Madison Square Garden as if it were their royal court. That magic was tangible to those who witnessed it, and was a catalyst in the lives of the players, changing the course of their fates forever.

With three seconds left on the clock and the score tied at 40, Utah's Herb Wilkinson knew time was running out. He could tell by the frantic look in the eyes of the Dartmouth defenders. For most of the game the Indians had maintained their elegant form, but now they were unhinged—almost tripping over themselves to get at the ball.

Bob Lewis had two men on him and was swinging his elbows from side to side to clear some space. He rose up wildly and saw Herb alone at the top of the key. With a flick of his wrists, the ball went sailing across the court and landed perfectly in Herb's hands.

Herb somehow found an opening in the smothering Dartmouth defense. Even though he was a step beyond the top of the key, he fixed his stance and raised his eyes toward the rim. The thought of the buzzer bore into Herb's mind, and he was sure it would end the spell that had carried them across the country to this unlikely place. Herb's gut reaction was to dish the ball to one of his teammates, but as he lifted the ball above his head and scanned the court he saw only a mass of defenders. Two of them turned toward him and he looked above their heads at the distant basket. It was his only choice. Herb's competitive instincts took over as he lofted the ball with a one-handed set shot. The screaming fans in sold-out Madison Square Garden fell silent as they witnessed the soft leather ball take flight and bounce gently on the iron rim.

The year was 1944 and the world kept watch on Europe and the Pacific for any indication of an Allied victory. In just three months the combined forces of the free world would launch their assault against the German forces at Normandy in France. The names Utah Beach and Omaha Beach would be thrust squarely into the forefront of the minds of all Americans. Families throughout the country, whose sons, fathers, husbands and brothers faced the enemy overseas, hoped that the dreaded letter from the War Department would pass them by.

In the Pacific, the war with Japan continued to take the lives of American solders. Thousands of American and Philippine soldiers continued to be held as prisoners of war by the Japanese in the Philippine Islands. Newsreels produced by the U.S. government focused on atrocities committed by the Japanese military against U.S. soldiers. More than 120,000 Japanese Americans lived as prisoners on American soil, held by a suspicious U.S. government in internment camps scattered throughout the western United States. Anti-Japanese sentiment in America was at a fevered level.

The focus of Americans, hungry for something to buoy their war-laden hearts, shifted from foreign conflicts to the culmination of one of the most unusual and dramatic stories in sports history. On the evening of March 28, 1944, in smoke-filled Madison Square Garden, the largest crowd ever assembled to watch a basketball game witnessed an event that elevated college basketball to the top of the nation's headlines. American soldiers tuned their radios to listen to the final game of the NCAA Tournament that pitted the unlikely University of Utah Utes against the heavily favored Dartmouth College Indians.

Dartmouth benefited from the addition of several stellar players enrolled at the school under the navy's wartime V-12 Program. The Utes, on the other hand, had to start four freshmen because their senior players were serving their country. The Utes were to have spent their season practicing and playing home games in the Einar Nielson Field House on the university campus, but it had been requisitioned by the army and converted into barracks, and so the Utes had to play their games in a church-owned gym in downtown Salt Lake City. They were not even supposed to appear in the NCAA Tournament. After losing to Kentucky in the National Invitation Tournament, a sudden tragedy for the University of Arkansas team opened a spot in the NCAA Tournament bracket and offered the Utah team a new opportunity. Because no one had anticipated the participation of the Utah team or their incredible tenacity, the media dubbed them the "Blitz Kids."

The tournament championship game stretched into overtime for the first time in NCAA history. After playing the entire game, the Utes' star freshman, Arnie Ferrin, was fighting exhaustion but played on. And in an irony only a war-torn country could understand, the tough New York crowd was standing and cheering for the intense defensive play of the spirited and tireless Wataru Misaka, a five-foot-seven-inch Japanese American who had been forced to play out of position at center due to an injury to the team's regular center, Fred Sheffield. For a few moments the country seemed to have forgotten its woes and fears as they united behind a team that by all rights shouldn't have even been playing in the championship game.

PROLOGUE

PAIN AND PROVIDENCE

Rolling down the window, University of Arkansas basketball coach Eugene Lambert felt the cool, moist air whip through his hair. The cold gusts caught in his throat, but he left the window down. On the radio he heard the Glenn Miller Orchestra. He cranked the knob and left the music playing a little too loudly. Neither the bitter wind nor the music could clear his mind, and there was nothing else he could do to steer his thoughts away from his task. Guided by the breeze from the window, his tears formed little trails that ran across his face toward his ears. Even these feeble efforts to distract himself had turned against him. Once again he caught himself looking at Deno Nichols's amputated leg wrapped in plastic, sitting on the passenger's seat next to him.

Coach Lambert didn't have many victories; in fact, he was only in his second year as head coach. He had high aspirations, though, and he often found himself in front of the glass-lined trophy case where the University of Arkansas honored its teams and athletes—a modern-day pantheon filled with glittering miniature monoliths. For Coach Lambert, standing in front of that case was as close as he could get to actually living those victories, as he tried to connect with the magic and greatness that had inspired former students and coaches.

He couldn't shake the mental picture of that trophy case from his mind as he looked at the plastic-wrapped thing on the seat next to him. His eyes were constantly drawn to it, and he couldn't help but think of it as some sort of ghastly reminder that instead of commemorating their accomplishments it represented all of their dashed dreams. It was a hellish abomination of a trophy, long and skinny, shining white in its plastic shroud. He had hoped to have a championship trophy to set in the passenger's seat as they returned, victorious, from the NCAA Tournament. Now they wouldn't even be going to Kansas City to participate in the tournament, and instead of a trophy, Coach Lambert had his star player's amputated leg as a passenger in his car.

It had taken everything he had to keep himself together the past few days. Since the accident, a mental battle had been going on in his soul as he fought to reconcile the uncontrollable events that had ended the Razorbacks' season, and more importantly, shattered the lives of several of his players and taken the life of a fellow teacher.

In his heart, Coach Lambert understood that a coach is more than just the guy who teaches players how to dribble the ball with each hand. He is a mentor, a guide who helps boys over the cusp to manhood. All of his drills, pep talks, everything he did as coach had a dual purpose: to make them better players for sure, but more importantly, to prepare them for life. He was responsible for helping them set the standards they would have for the rest of their lives, and now this abomination stood as a reminder of how wrong things had gone.

Instead of the victory parade he had secretly hoped for, he now drove out of town, a one-man caravan, to find a proper place for a burial. The doctor who had given the leg to him suggested he put it in the trunk, but that didn't feel right. So it sat in the front seat next to him.

Just four days earlier, Saturday, March 18, 1944, Coach Lambert had scheduled a pretournament tune-up game against the Camp Chaffee Tankers. It had started out a close game, but the Razorbacks ultimately lost to the team from Fort Smith, 58–42. After the game, Coach Lambert stayed with the second team, who were going to play against another team at the base. He sent his tired starting five home with Everett Norris, a physical education instructor at the university. By chance, Coach Lambert had seen Everett on campus earlier that day and asked if he would be willing to drive the boys home after the practice game. It had been the first opportunity Everett had had to travel with the team, and he had happily agreed.

It had also been the first game for the new center on the team, six-foot-ten-inch giant George Kok from Michigan. Coach Lambert had heard about him playing in an amateur league and sent him a letter offering him a college education and a chance to improve his game. After his first practice with the team, George was put in the starting five. A set of bunk beds were disassembled and put back together, end-to-end, to create the only bed on campus long enough for George to sleep on. That Saturday also happened to be his birthday.

Rounding out an already good team, George fit in well with the two stars, Deno Nichols and Ben Jones. The team's conference record was good at 16–7. With the addition of a man who could get tangled in the net if he jumped too high, they were planning on a big splash as the Southwest Conference representative in the NCAA Tournament that was just a few days away.

The drive home from the game took Everett Norris and the first team along a meandering eighty-mile stretch of Route 71. The world was a soggy mess from a day full of indecisive storms. Everything was just a mash of brights and darks as they traveled along the soaked two-lane highway.

Crammed with five lanky players and one teacher, the maroon, wood-paneled station wagon sauntered its way up a sloping hill when a loud "boom" startled the tired players from their post-game dozing. Since the shoulders of the road were rivers of mud, Everett had no choice but to stop the car on the road. They all quickly got out, and both Deno and Ben, the leaders of the team both on and off the court, helped Everett as he started to replace the flat tire.

After grabbing a flashlight, George and a teammate, Red Wheeler, stood beside the car to warn the oncoming traffic. Waving his light in the air as a few cars slowed down and passed by, George laughed as someone joked that he looked like a lighthouse towering over the road. However they were all a little uneasy being in the middle of the highway on such a night, and George got a little nervous each time a new pair of headlights appeared over the hill.

They worked as fast as their cold, wet hands would allow, and soon most of the players were piling back into the station wagon. Everett,

Deno and Ben finished attaching the old tire to the back of the car. George and Red were walking back to the car when George noticed another pair of headlights cresting the hill behind them.

George spun back around to face the oncoming car and repeated his nervous wave while calling out, but it was as if he were invisible. The lights were still coming straight at him. He waved the light again and dread filled his chest as the ghostly pair of shining eyes gained speed. Frozen by fear, he had no time to think about what was happening. At the last second he was brought to his senses when Red shouted "Jump!" George looked to the others as he flung himself out of the way.

There was no screeching sound, just a sickening thud as the car plowed into the back of the station wagon. As he slammed against the muddy embankment, George caught a glimpse of Ben Jones flying through the air.

Still operating on instinct, George clambered up the muddy embankment to his friends. What he saw was more than he could handle. He felt himself go numb as he saw Deno and Everett lying on the pavement between the cars, both writhing in pain. Deno's right leg bent unnaturally to the side and a shattered shard of bone stuck out through his pants leg. Both of Ben's legs were covered with blood and he lay on his back screaming. It looked like Everett was bent over when the car had crushed him. He was alive and awake, but he had been split wide open from his pelvis to his chest.

The driver of the other car, a local mortician named Maurice Russell, emerged from his car with his wife, his hand on his head. With eyes wide as dinner plates, his wife put her hand to her mouth to muffle a cry.

A mishmash of cries and shouts were exchanged as the uninjured jumped into action. There wasn't a service station or phone for miles around, so they decided to load the injured into the damaged but still functioning station wagon and head for the hospital ten miles away in Fayetteville. They tore the seats from the rear of the wagon, but getting Ben and Deno in was torture. Neither could support his own weight, so every step they were carried multiplied their agony.

As the cause of so much suffering, Maurice felt that he had to help, so he assisted in removing the back seat and moving the injured players. As they lugged the moaning boys to the car, George caught a whiff of Maurice's breath. He was certain Maurice smelled of alcohol.

It took three of them to move Ben alone. Deno could put weight on one leg. Everett's massive injuries made it unbearable for him to lie down, so he sat in the front seat supported by Mike Schumchyk, the only uninjured player to get back in the car.

With no obvious injuries except for a sizable goose egg on his forehead, Maurice took the wheel of the makeshift ambulance and headed for the hospital. For the rest of the trip the only sounds in the car were the groans of a man and two boys, passengers to an improvised chauffeur—an undertaker, no less—who had pulverized their bodies and destroyed their dreams. The only words spoken were from Mike in the front seat, who only a few hours earlier had been rallying his teammates on the court. Now all he could do was urge them to hang on.

With no room for them in the station wagon, Red and George had no choice but to stay behind and wait for Coach Lambert and the other players to show up following their second game of the night. Not knowing what else to do, George, still armed with his flashlight, panned the asphalt in front of the wrecked car and saw bits of bone among the splashes of blood that were slowly being washed away in the rain. Thinking that they might be needed later, he picked them up and set them on the smashed hood of the car.

All around them the world reflected their tragedy. Fog clouded their vision and heavy drops of rain fell. It wasn't long before both boys were shivering from the cold. Not much was said between them as they stared at the mangled car in the road. Mrs. Russell urged them to join her in the car and get out of the rain, but they chose to stay out in the cold, knowing they couldn't escape the bitter chill that filled them.

Time passed slowly and they had nothing else to do but relive those few life-changing moments. Again and again they saw those two bright lights grow bigger and bigger, followed by the thud that caused George to shudder each time it played in his mind. Eventually George lost himself in time, stuck between those two lights.

A police car approached from the direction Maurice had driven off in and slowed to a stop in front of them. The sheriff walked over to where George and Red were standing. Maurice, who had ridden back in the police car, got out and walked over to his car. Without saying a word to anyone, he got in and drove off with his wife. Perplexed, George turned to the sheriff.

"That man's been drinking!" he said, louder than expected.

Peering out from under his hat, the sheriff responded, "Boy, I know Mr. Russell and he ain't a drinkin' man." With that, the investigation into what happened that night was concluded.

Back in Fayetteville, Everett Norris was pronounced dead from massive shock and internal injuries. Both Deno and Ben were in critical condition, and doctors worked to stabilize their injuries. Ben's spine had been fractured in several places, and he'd suffered compound fractures above both of his ankles. He was transferred to another hospital better equipped to handle his severe injuries. Deno appeared to be better off, with only his right leg damaged—although severely. There were compound fractures in two different places and extensive tissue damage caused by the impact of the car and the shattered bones. Doctors decided that any attempt to set his fractures would be too risky, since he was still in severe shock. They chose to leave his mangled leg alone until his condition improved.

George and Red, still out in the cold, waited by the road until the coach and the rest of the team caught up. When Coach Lambert finally drove up and spotted two of his players by the side of the road next to a smashed car, he slammed on the brakes and lurched out of his car toward the two blood-streaked boys. His face was twisted in confusion and then horror as he saw the pool of blood running off the road. The whole thing was too much for George, and the story spilled out of him in one breathless sob.

For the first time as head coach, Coach Lambert was at a loss for words. He always had an anecdote or lesson to teach in any situation, be it victory or loss. But here, soaking in the bitter, wet cold, he broke down in front of his boys, as tears joined the streams of rain running down his face. George and Red squeezed into the car with their teammates and headed for home. One by one, Coach Lambert walked his players to their doors before he drove to the hospital.

It was past 4:00 a.m. when George finally laid down in his bed, but he couldn't sleep. Every time he turned the lights out he began replaying the accident. Time and time again he saw Ben flying through the air. He lay in his improvised bed with the lights on for hours just staring at the ceiling.

Early the next morning, Coach Lambert announced Arkansas's withdrawal from the NCAA Basketball Tournament. There had been talk of going on in a show of honor, but Eugene knew that was no more than grand gesturing. Sure, the idea of winning it all after such a tragedy seemed poetic, but the coach knew that they didn't stand a chance without their two stars. And in comparison to what his boys were going through, the tournament was trivial.

He had urged his players all season to stay focused on their goals. He did everything he could to make sure they didn't let their actions off the court and away from school get in the way of their game. But fate had interceded. What happened on Route 71 eclipsed any thought of basketball. And though Eugene knew it wasn't his fault, he couldn't stand the idea that something off the court had brought their whole season crashing down.

By Tuesday the doctors realized the full extent of Deno's injuries. He had complained of severe pain, but it wasn't until a visiting doctor noted a high fever and a putrid smell that drastic plans had to be made if they were going to save his life. The massive tissue damage and loss of blood to his lower leg had provided a breeding ground for infection, and gangrene was already ravaging his tissues. Most likely he would die within forty-eight hours unless his leg were amputated.

Virginia Nichols, Deno's wife of just a few weeks, rushed to the hospital when she heard the news. Deno's parents were already there. The family lingered in the hallway and discussed the details in hushed voices. Deno didn't know exactly what was going on, but he guessed that his life as he had known it was about to end in any case.

Virginia didn't have the heart to tell him the news she knew would crush him. Deno was the Southwest Conference's leading scorer and was known for his stunning ball-handling skills. He loved football and swimming and had found a passion for dancing with his new bride. What would he have left with all that taken away? Virginia knew that Deno was going to lose more than just his leg—if he survived.

She stayed in the waiting area as Deno's father went to tell his son what the doctors had decided. She couldn't even bring herself to watch her father-in-law walk down the hallway. Instead, she sat on the floor, hugged her legs and listened breathlessly as the click-clack of his shoes faded. Once he entered Deno's room, there was silence . . . and then a scream.

At a nearby hospital, Ben had both of his legs set. Luckily there were no signs of infection. But because of the severity of his injuries, only one of his half-dozen doctors gave him any chance of ever walking again.

A day after Deno's surgery, Coach Lambert came to the hospital to present Deno with his letterman's jacket. The coach's heart was still broken; he couldn't bring himself to even look at the cameraman from the university paper as they posed for a photo. All he could do was stare at Deno lying awkwardly in his hospital bed, the sheets flat where a leg should have been. He held Deno's hand, but there was simply nothing he could say.

The picture that ran in the school paper showed Deno and his wife staring blankly at the camera. While he had survived the accident, Deno was already moving slowly toward his grave. He cancelled the contract he had signed just a week earlier to coach football and basketball at North Little Rock High School. Virginia knew he would recover physically, but she also knew that his will to live had gone with his leg.

A fidgety doctor caught Coach Lambert on the way out of the hospital. He had a favor to ask. This was a small hospital and they weren't used to dealing with things like this. They had no idea what to do with Deno's leg.

As he escorted the leg out of town, Coach Lambert sobbed and wiped the tears from his cheeks. There was no sense to what happened, and nothing could change it. He wasn't thinking about what the team could have accomplished, but rather what the accident had done to his boys and Everett.

After driving for thirty minutes and finding a beautiful place in the trees, Eugene pulled to the side of the road. Looking around and finding himself alone, he tenderly lifted the plastic-wrapped leg from the front seat and walked to the back of the car to retrieve a shovel from the trunk. This would be a quiet, solitary funeral. The coach knelt in the soft Arkansas earth and dug a hole for Deno's leg. His tears fell onto ground still moist from the stormy weekend.

How could he have known that from the University of Arkansas's private tragedy a phoenix would arise—the greatest underdog in the history of college basketball. A young Cinderella team from Utah was poised to take advantage of that tragedy and turn it into an unlikely dream come true.

WATARU

Ability is a poor man's wealth.

—JOHN WOODEN

Rays of light glinted off the amber beer bottle as it spun through the trees and into the alley. An unsuspecting young pass-erby with a streak of midnight black hair barely had time to dodge the missile as it shattered in the alley, shards of glass dancing across the crumbled cement where they came to rest among tin cans and sun-bleached newspapers. The alcoholic bombardier's only intended victim was his bottle, but he was nonetheless thrilled at the surprised boy and the scene he had created. Slurred laughter bounced off the mottled brick walls as the young boy, Wat Misaka, darted down the street, blending into the surroundings as he was accustomed to doing.

In the 1930s, Ogden's 25th Street was more than just a thoroughfare leading from the railroad station to downtown. In a state known for its moral fortitude, 25th Street was the capital of all things unprincipled. Quaint exteriors showed a bright face to the street, but a few feet below the bustling sidewalks a hidden world thrived. A series of underground rooms and tunnels connected the length of the "Two-Bit District";

some of these interconnected rooms originally functioned as storage spaces for the businesses above, but were converted for more profitable ventures. Respectable people could enter a bank, descend a hidden stairway and disappear into a seedy underground world of opium dens and prosperous brothels. Rumors persisted of a hand-dug tunnel that ran several blocks north, fashioned by hard-working bootleggers preserving their profession during Prohibition. And the hand of depravity stretched toward the east as well, fed by these arterial underground tunnels that connected the red-light district in an unseen web.

The Misaka family sprouted out of the same musky earth that provided safe passage for prostitutes and gamblers. Underneath his 25th Street barbershop, Ben Misaka carved a home out of dirt walls and a dirt floor.

The year was 1902 when Fusaichi Misaka resolved to escape the life of a farmer and leave the small Japanese island of Iwashi-Jima to follow an acquaintance to America. Leaving his homeland was the first step in his new life; the next step was leaving his name behind as well. As Fusaichi, he had been an orphan, destined to live his days wrestling with the land. After arriving in America, Fusaichi would forever be known as Ben. Now he would mold a new life and have a family of his own. He abandoned the sickle to pick up shears and a straight-edge razor.

Ben bought a small barbershop from a Greek immigrant in Ogden, Utah. He could have chosen San Francisco or other California cities with sizable Japanese immigrant populations, but instead he settled in Utah because he thought it might be safer. A small population of Japanese immigrants had sprung up around Ogden, providing a small network of support, not to mention the prospects of a reliable clientele who spoke his native tongue. The barbershop was surrounded by taverns and located less than a block from the railroad depot in Ogden. Proximity to transportation theoretically meant a steady stream of customers, which all too often unfortunately turned into a mere trickle.

For several years Ben pined away in loneliness, until eventually he had saved enough money to take a few weeks off work and return to Japan to find a bride. Though poor by American standards, as an owner of his own business in America he seemed quite the catch to the girls in the Japanese village he grew up in.

There wasn't time or money for a honeymoon, so Ben and his new wife, Tatsuyo, returned to America immediately to start their new lives together. It wasn't long after that they learned they were expecting their first child. After hundreds of years of a proud Japanese lineage, their son Wataru was the first Misaka child born in America.

Wataru's first few years were spent crawling around the feet of his father's barbershop customers, playing amidst the locks of hair on the floor. Being constantly exposed to English speakers, he developed an ease with the language that his parents lacked. By the time he started school he sounded like a regular American kid.

On his first day of class, his name was shortened to "Wat." He and his two younger brothers would continue the name-altering tradition started by their father, doing so more out of convenience rather than any overt attempt to assimilate themselves. Wat's younger brother Tatsumi became "Tats"; Osamu, the youngest child, adopted the moniker "Oscar"; and even their mother was called "Mary" on some occasions.

Slow times meant that both chairs in the small barbershop were often empty. On the rare occasion when there was more than one customer, Ben manned them both. About a dozen feet into the shop, Ben constructed a wall that separated the two halves of his life—work and family. On the family side was a small stove, sink and a set of stairs that led to rooms below where the Misakas lived. It was behind that wall that Tatsuyo struggled to keep the rest of the family's life in order. Not a customer passed through the shop without seeing Ben meticulously mopping the glistening floor to preserve the pristine appearance of his little shop. Behind the rear wall, he was just as strict. With his family, he felt a great need to maintain order and discipline, especially with his children. It took everything he had to keep his family from the brink of poverty, and he struggled to balance those two worlds under one roof.

However, he had his jovial side too. On Saturdays, friends and acquaintances would gather in Ben's shop, where they would receive discounted haircuts and an endless stream of conversation. Mostly they just came for a sense of community, which is so hard to find when one is so far from home. People would even come on trains from nearby cities to spend the day chatting in the barbershop, making it—for one day a week, at least—the hub of northern Utah's Japanese community.

Times were tough, and it always seemed as if there was never quite enough money for Ben and his family, so those busy Saturdays were crucial to them being able to make it through the rest of the week.

The Misakas might have been poor, but the three boys were completely unaware of it. Having grown up in the midst of pool halls and taverns, the three felt completely at home. They learned to adjust to oddities that to them were daily occurrences. They recognized that some women in the neighborhood wore vastly different clothing, but the boys did not grasp the concept of their illicit occupation. Bars and drunks were to be avoided, and there was an unspoken understanding that the boys were not to venture out onto the main street after dark.

Amid the chaos the children did find a way to remain children, almost unaware of the adult world that surrounded them. Just a stick and a ball were required to transform them into baseball heroes, and basketball hoops were made out of anything remotely round. The alleyways were their own little kingdoms, filled with hidden corners that made prime hiding spots allowing them to become champions at kick the can. Their only toy was a little red wagon, which they towed to Brown's Ice Cream Shop every day to buy a block of ice for the icebox at home. Their cargo rested on a gunnysack to prevent it from sliding out of the wagon as they raced home.

Their doting father indulged the boys with his love of baseball. His short stature and heavy frame prevented him from venturing onto the diamond, but it didn't prevent him from living his dreams through his children. When Tats hit a home run during a game, his father was so pleased he rewarded him with a dollar—the same amount as their monthly water bill. On Sundays, he would often take the boys to the nearby baseball field to watch local teams play. Ben rallied neighborhood children together to play an early urban version of the game. A world away from his homeland, Ben had found what he never knew as a child, and he let these rambunctious boys create their own world within, but wholly apart from, the harsh reality around them.

Neither Ben nor Tatsuyo had mastered the English language, so family friends tutored Wat instead. Before he started first grade, he was taught to read and write in English and had a head start in math. A neighboring Japanese family ran a boarding house, the Western, a few blocks from Ben's barbershop. Their children were older, but they were also their family's first generation born in America. As with many Japanese Americans, the two families watched out for and took care of each other.

His informal preschooling gave Wat an advantage over his classmates from the first bell, and he would continue his academic excellence throughout the rest of his education. Wat quickly made friends, and soon he and three of his pals wandered the Two-Bit District as the Four Musketeers. The four would remain friends for life.

It wasn't until elementary school that Wat was formally introduced to basketball. On the playground of Grant Elementary School, two basketball standards stood towering above a dirt court. Wat and his young friends were transported to a place where time had no meaning as they played those early games. Once the sun went down, the game was moved to an improvised court in a nearby lighted alleyway. They took their playtime seriously, and didn't mind the wet hands and soggy shoes that accompanied winter play.

Even though basketball was still a relatively young sport in the 1930s and '40s, it had permeated every corner of the country. It had fulfilled one of its original purposes, which was to provide a game to play indoors during the winter months. Its popularity had grown to the point where it was played by tens of thousands of people across the country.

It had a particular grip on Utahans, and not just the young ones. LDS Church buildings throughout the state added basketball standards to their indoor gyms to encourage healthy activity. Where there were no indoor gyms, they simply nailed a hoop to a wall. Basketball was so popular among Mormons that every congregation had a team of young men and competed in tournaments. The majority of the state population belonged to the LDS Church, which guaranteed the church teams got as much attention in the papers as many of the state's college teams.

Large swaths of the state were sparsely populated, and in those parts of the state where communities were small and distractions few, the game of basketball blossomed because it only required a peach basket, a barn, and a ball. In many cities, leagues were formed and teams assembled.

Several teams were formed at Hill Field, a new military installation near Ogden. The sizable Japanese American population in northern Utah even formed some leagues of their own.

Summers weren't spent idly; the days were long and tedious as Wat helped out on his relatives' nearby farm, which also allowed him to save some money for his future. Wat was out of bed and on his bicycle before the sun crested the tall mountains to the east. The bike ride to the farm went from his home on 25th Street out to 2nd Street, on the northern edge of Ogden. He toiled like any farmhand, picking peas and tomatoes, weeding, digging, hauling manure and performing every other imaginable form of labor. His bike would carry him home only after the sun finished its arc across the desert sky. A weekly reprieve came every Sunday, when he would leave at five to play in Ogden's Japanese Baseball League.

The Misaka family wasn't able to provide their sons many luxuries, so Wat's sporting equipment consisted of nothing more than his arms and legs. He played year-round, bouncing from sport to sport depending on the season. In the alley behind his house, he dug a small pit that he filled with hay. A few sticks and a bamboo pole were reborn as a high-jump standard for Wat, which allowed him to practice his scissors kick. During his two years at Central Junior High School, he also tried his hand at tennis, swimming, track and football.

Athletic prowess made Wat an excellent young quarterback, but his small frame made him vulnerable. Running a quarterback sneak in one game, he injured his shoulder badly when he was run over by a train posing as a linebacker. The opposing player had timed the tackle perfectly, engulfing Wat in a mass of flesh and shoulder pads. On the sidelines, someone quickly improvised a sling and Wat made his way home. Going to the hospital was an expense that he didn't want his family to endure, so he tried to convince himself that his injury was minor. Three days later the pain hadn't let up, helping Wat's decision to forgo a career in football.

Knowing a little about Wat's life, Central basketball coach Harold Welch sought him out and took him under his wing. He made some arrangements, and before long Wat was on his way to the hospital, where his collarbone was set and his dislocated shoulder reduced and put back into the socket where it belonged. Coach Welch saw something in Wat. He had speed, guile and determination that set him apart from other kids his age. After his injury, Wat had no plans to ever don football gear again, so with the encouragement of the coach, he joined the Central Junior High basketball squad.

During the fall of 1938, Wat and the rest of the Central basketball team celebrated a monumental victory, beating three other teams in a local basketball tournament. As with most junior high teams, watching the Cubs play was like watching an accident with time-outs. Offensive play was no more advanced than a slot machine: plug away long enough and with some luck you might just win something. Their defense was not much more complicated but easier to implement: choose the nearest opponent and stick to him like lint on a sweater. The boys ran a lot, but they had no idea where they were going or how they were going to get there.

The game of basketball still had some growing up to do too. There was no such thing as a three-pointer, let alone a slam dunk. Players were urged to keep their feet firmly on the ground when making shots, as many people thought jumping would decrease their accuracy. It was standard practice at all levels of basketball that coaches were not allowed to speak to their players during the games—even during time-outs—leaving the players to huddle together by themselves on the court and bumble their way through four quarters with minimal guidance. In spite of the juvenile rules, Wat rose above the adolescent mediocrity and showed real promise.

The life that Ben Misaka had constructed for his family was all that he could have hoped for when he left his homeland. Unfortunately, that life would be short-lived. On a windy night in the spring of 1939, Ben followed his parents into an early grave as his family gathered around his hospital bed. The doctor's explanation was kidney failure. Suddenly Tatsuyo, who was twenty years younger than Ben, was forced to reassess her family's place in America.

From the minute she had arrived in America, Tatsuyo had been the unseen hand that held the family and business together. For years she had labored behind the scenes, on the other side of the wall, hidden from Ben's barbershop customers. Consequently she spoke little

English, and knew even less about cutting hair or shaving men's faces. The obvious solution was to do what was easiest: Tatsuyo's brother had offered her family a place in the home their parents left to him back in Japan. Young Wat couldn't imagine leaving the only country he had ever known to go live on a small island where no one spoke his language. He was so determined to stay that he told his mother to take his two younger brothers and return to her homeland without him. At fifteen years of age, he felt he would find a way to make it on his own. This tactic inadvertently worked to convince Tatsuyo that their family needed to face their future together in America, if only for the sake of her children.

Tatsuyo would spend the rest of her life trying to be the disciplinarian that her late husband had been. But more often than not, her warm heart prevented her from acting even remotely authoritative. Life, and her stubborn eldest son, left her no choice but to venture out in front of the back wall to pick up the shears her husband had left behind. Her sons were the first unwilling victims of her shaky and unproven hands. They bore the brunt of her stylistic experiments and the full force of her learning curve, but at least they weren't paying customers. Never in her life had she entertained the thought that she would have to be the breadwinner for her family. The needs of her three boys provided an escape from her sorrow and forced her to work her way through her loss. With her hair combed neatly and wound into a tight bun, she would don a pristine white apron. To her customers she was positive and friendly, yet always reserved in her demeanor. She quickly fell into her new role, and her customers never suspected that they were under the blade of a novice.

As the oldest child, Wat had to bear the family loss by learning how to wash, iron and cook. Saturdays were busy in the barbershop, where the smell of menthol mingled with the beefy aromas of stew wafting from Wat's rudimentary kitchen creations. Sundays were spent cleaning the barbershop and sharpening scissors. Just as he had learned to survive in Ogden's hostile Two-Bit District, Wat learned to act in some ways as a father figure to his brothers and other neighborhood children. There was little money for toys or other childhood distractions, but Wat made a point of saving a few dimes to spend on gifts for his brothers and the neighbor's children who lived in the apartment above the barbershop. One Christmas morning Wat's brothers were thrilled to find a small stack of Dick Tracy comics waiting for them under the Christmas tree. The simple tag on their precious gift read "From Santa."

Tatsuyo insisted that her children be allowed to continue to be children and not be overwhelmed by the extra burdens they had to bear. She knew that the death of their father had forced them to grow up prematurely, but she did not want them to miss out on all the joys of childhood. As crushing as losing his father was, Wat still relished the joys of youth. Childish invention circumnavigated any obstacles that poverty threw in his path. Instead of paying to ski on the slopes at the new Snowbasin Resort, Wat and his friend Roy Yoshioka made the foothills above Ogden High School their own private ski resort, using skis that were no more than wooden slats with straps to hold their feet.

In Japanese tradition, the eldest son is the sole heir to all that the parents have and is considered the head of the household in the absence of a father. Tatsuyo would close up shop early on game days to prepare a meal in honor of Wat before he headed off to his basketball games. Wat's new role as a father figure was amplified by the age differences between the three boys. Wat was five years older than his nearest brother, Tats, and eight years older than Oscar. The two younger boys stuck together and looked up to their older brother, who lived in an almost entirely different sphere, busy with things that didn't interest them yet.

During Wat's second year at Central, his basketball team went undefeated in its six-game season. The championship game win over Mound Fort Junior High was big enough news to merit a four-column photograph of the youngsters on the sports page of the local *Ogden Standard-Examiner*. Three of the Four Musketeers were in the picture: one sat in front sheepishly holding the team jersey, and another kneeled bare-chested while proudly flashing a toothy grin. In the middle was Wat, a reserved smile on his face.

The *Standard-Examiner*'s sports editor, Al Warden, attended the game and took an interest in the young players. He noted, "forwards Pete Ramirez and Wat Misaka were two of the cleverest ball hawks the team had on tap." Pete may have been the debonair one of their group, but Wat had the brains and the determination. The Musketeers were inseparable and constantly competing in sports, but they steadily relied on Wat for help in their studies. Upon first glance, few would guess the surprising abilities of this short, quiet young man. Wat felt that his actions reflected on his family, and he made sure that one could only infer the best things from the way he acted. Once he donned his basketball togs, his quiet strength was hard to ignore.

During his first year of high school, Wat's duties toward his family were heavier than ever, forcing him to shoulder the loss of his father both emotionally and responsibly. But his loss didn't show on the basketball court. He continued to attract his coach's attention. As was common at the time, most offensive action was improvised, as the players decided themselves how best to make plays. Basketball strategy centered on the ability of the players to think on their feet as the defense came at them. This meant that a player's role on the team could change from game to game. During some games Wat was one of the leading scorers on the team; on other nights he would spend most of his time supporting his teammates from the bench. In spite of the higher caliber of play compared to his junior high career, Wat fared well due to his tenacity and stamina. After his summers of hard labor on his relatives' farm, Wat was muscular and quick with impressive endurance. Playing four quarters of basketball without a substitution felt no more exhausting than a walk through an orchard.

Ogden High School coach Gilbert "Moe" Moesinger saw enough promise in Wat during his junior year to have him travel with the varsity team and substitute for the senior players on occasion. Wat's contributions to Ogden High's win in the state championship game his first year were minimal—he scored just one point—but he was a significant part of the only team in the school's century-long history to have won the championship. During his senior year, he and fellow guard Max Jensen would share the spotlight as they battled for the honor of the team's leading scorer.

During his final year in high school the team won its regional championship and was expected to take the state championship again, but was caught off guard in the first game of the state tournament against Davis High and settled for seventh place. Wat also spent time honing his skills in the local Japanese American basketball leagues, after all his school work and family responsibilities had been taken care of. He continued playing in the leagues even after his high school career was over and he'd begun his studies at Weber College.

Wat never showed much interest in politics or current events. But on the first Sunday in December, 1941, Wat found himself alone in the barbershop, cleaning, as the radio brought the news that would make the world seem much smaller: Japan had bombed Pearl Harbor. Scared and not knowing what else to do, he called his aunt's house where his mother was. She calmed him and advised him not to leave the house for the rest of the day.

Wat was saddened by the horrible news that crackled over the radio, as all Americans were, but his sadness was mingled with apprehension. Japan was his parents' homeland, but he didn't feel any affection for the recent actions of that country, and definitely didn't want to be connected to the horrible events that had occurred an ocean away. From that moment on, however, the world treated him differently.

For years, oceans had separated the world's battles from American soil. The suffering that most Americans had only read about in newspapers was suddenly painfully real. The war had been brought home and the country struggled to understand how to deal with it. In the Misaka home, it took several days before the children returned to school. On his first day back, Wat saw two Hawaiian schoolmates beside themselves with worry. Not a word was spoken between them, but Wat felt their resentment through their silence. When he walked down the street in front of his home, passersby glared at him and shouted to get out of their way.

Wat didn't know it then, but the bombs that were dropped thousands of miles away had sent shock waves across the world that would change everything.

ARNIE

I am sure that no man can derive more pleasure from money or power
than I do from seeing a pair of basketball goals in some out of the way
place—deep in the Wisconsin woods an old barrel hoop nailed to a tree, or
a weather-beaten shed on the Mexican border with a rusty iron hoop nailed
to one end.

—JAMES NAISMITH

As he read the list hanging on the door of the gym at
Central Junior High School, Arnie unwittingly joined in an American
tradition. He read the roster more than once, just to make sure he
hadn't missed his name the first time—but no, he had been cut from
the ninth-grade basketball team. Disappointment caught in his throat
and hung in his chest as he turned and began his walk home.

That same sense of sadness has been felt by thousands of
American youth, legions of children cut from teams who sense that
some sort of injustice has occurred. They say to themselves, "I should
have made the team." Like them, Arnie reviewed the plays he made
during tryouts, the shots he had missed and what he could have done
differently. Just like those who had passed this road before, he tried
to find a way to absolve himself and pacify his disappointment. Arnie

resolved that the coach had simply made a wrong decision; he had failed to notice Arnie's obvious athletic prowess. Fate had simply dealt him a bad hand. It was not his fault. Though his wishes were the same as so many others', Arnie's unusual determination would soon set him apart. That and the fact that he was already six feet four inches tall in the ninth grade.

The fall sunset in Utah turned the sky orange and draped the valley in a blanket of warm autumn hues. The homes that surrounded Ogden High School glowed with an earthy light as Arnie walked home. The fact that he was cut from the team would not change what he was going to do when he got home. He walked those few blocks, picked up his basketball and started shooting baskets.

Rich fall colors eventually gave way to wintry grays, but Arnie kept shooting baskets, even shoveling snow off the driveway and continuing his one-man tournament through the ensuing winter months. The last rays of winter sun often found him shooting a stiff leather ball with frosted fingers numbed from the cold.

Arnie's unusual dedication to the game came in part from a pure love of the sport. Even years earlier one could have spotted the budding athlete and his love for the game. Some of his earliest memories were from his parent's first home in Ogden's east bench—a Victorian mansion that sported a basketball court on the third floor. Another reason for his dedication was his improvised family. His mother died when he was only three years old, and Arnie's father, who shared a name with his son (but was known as just "Arn"), buried his sorrows in his work. And there was plenty to lose himself in. He owned a service station and a small home oil delivery company. Eventually he was away on business more often than he was home. After losing the love of his life, Arn decided that he didn't have the time nor the aptitude to be a single parent. He loved his son, but deferred his parental responsibilities to his own parents.

The only tie that remained between Arnie and his mother was a small scrapbook she had made for him before her death. He read the book, often for hours at a time, hoping to find a stronger connection with her. The green leather book was well crafted and showed the love a dying mother held for her only child. The pages were filled with small black-and-white photographs of Arnie as a baby posing with his parents. Each had a small caption indicating the place and people in the photo. Since he was only three when she died, his memories of her had faded. The vague memories that remained were stimulated by those photos and an active imagination.

Arnie's grandparents, Ida and Chariton Phillip Ferrin, stepped in to fill the void in his life. They took him into their home and loved him and made every effort to create a family for him. They raised him as any grandparent would, adoring and supporting him. Ida was fifty-one years of age when she rededicated her life to providing every opportunity for Arnie as if he were her own son, though at times she struggled to find the strength and endurance needed for rearing an active child. She approached her responsibilities toward Arnie as a stewardship and she tried her best to nurture him and fulfill the role of a substitute mother. Arnie's grandfather, C. P., managed a service station that he owned with his son, Arn, and worked hard to support Ida and Arnie and provide a home.

Being a generation removed from current children's fashion trends, Ida dressed Arnie in dress slacks and shirts, shined leather shoes and a tie. School pictures featured his friends dressed in coveralls, farm shirts and secondhand Converse Chuck Taylor All-Stars. In addition to his distinctive clothing, Ida's health-conscious lunch selections led Arnie to exclude himself from the ritual lunchtime barter.

Arnie's elevated stature and outdated wardrobe were not the only reasons he received attention from his schoolmates. He also had an unusual name. His given name was Chariton Arnold Ferrin Jr. Although he was proud of his first name, he tried to keep it secret in fear that his schoolmates would think Chariton sounded "girly." Arnie's great-grandfather was born to Mormon pioneers following their flight from Nauvoo, Illinois. In the mid-1800s they had established a semipermanent campsite along the Chariton River in southern Iowa. In memory of the safety they found in that quiet haven, Arnie's ancestors named their first-born son Chariton. Arnie, his father, grandfather and great-grandfather all proudly carried that name from their predecessor.

Despite the devastating loss of his mother at an early age, Arnie was rambunctious as a child and wore a smile often enough that friends and family nicknamed him "Sunny Boy." He had enough energy for his giant frame and a little extra. In spite of all his quirkiness, Arnie had a cadre of friends. Without a brother or sister, however, he often found himself at home alone and a little lonely. But all he had to do was pick up his basketball and he felt content once again.

Basketball was still a young sport in the 1930s. James Naismith had created the game just over forty years earlier, and it was played in the Olympics for the first time as an official medal event in 1936. It had spread across the nation and was already taking root across the globe. Basketball was an American ritual. In rural western states, most barns, sheds or garages provided support for rudimentary basketball hoops that would rally youngsters. Arnie was lucky to have an official basketball hoop with a net that was attached to the garage just to the side of the home where he lived with his grandparents. Having a wide driveway was a luxury that provided Arnie the opportunity to practice shooting the ball from many different angles and distances.

At the time, basketballs were handmade from smooth leather, with seams running along the exterior, segmenting the ball like an orange. After countless hours practicing in his driveway, Arnie's ball lost its sheen and the seams started to split. C. P. got him a new ball and installed a light on the side of the house so Arnie could keep playing after dark. He worked his way through several balls, shooting from every square inch of the driveway. When he discovered a weakness in his shot, he would repeat it until he improved. He took on countless imaginary adversaries and learned to dribble the ball with his left hand just as well as he could with his right. He learned to shoot at the hoop from every angle and repeated the shots until they were as natural to him as walking. Beyond his concrete arena, time and the world faded away until Arnie had created his own microcosm that he had complete control over.

Upon first glance, Arnie didn't appear to be anything close to an athlete. No amount of Ida's home cooking could add a single pound to his thin frame. He appeared to be little more than bone and skin with a healthy mop of blond hair. He had sprouted at such a young age it was difficult for him to keep up with his own size. In elementary school, a teacher encouraged him, saying she thought he was the best athlete in the school. At the end of the year, Arnie was thrilled to put himself to a test. He entered the fifty-yard dash on Field Day, and with his teacher's words in mind, expected to dominate his schoolmates. The first day, Arnie ran in a heat that he knew would provide little challenge. He took a decisive second. The second day he competed against his best friend's little sister, Donna, and to his horror she blew by Arnie like he was running uphill in a river. On his report card that term Arnie received all A's—except for one P (for "poor") in physical performance. A fine grade, he thought, for the "best athlete in the school."

Arnie was eleven years old when his father started dating again. On his infrequent trips home, Arn would mention a woman from a small town just north of Ogden. It wasn't long before Arnie heard his grandparents talking about Arn and Lu's marriage. They seemed pleased that Arn had found someone with whom to share his life. They talked of a grand house to be built on twenty acres of land in the southern part of Ogden where Arnie could play, ride horses and enjoy all the opportunities he could imagine. Having shared the love and home of Ida and C. P. from the time his mother passed away until his father remarried, Arnie knew no other family. He loved them as much as any child could love a parent. Arn's frequent absences from home for work responsibilities had caused him and Arnie to drift apart. Had he been given the choice of staying with Ida and C. P. or moving into his father's estate in the southern part of Ogden, there is no doubt that Arnie would have stayed with his grandparents in their modest home. But he didn't have to make that decision; his father made it for him. He had a room at Arn's house, but he only visited.

Ida and C. P. couldn't ignore Arnie's precocious athleticism and C. P. took every opportunity to help Arnie improve. Just before his fourteenth birthday, Arnie took a trip with C. P. to Detroit to buy a new car. Buying one directly from the factory allowed them to save more than enough money to pay for the trip and have some fun on the way home. After they purchased the new Pontiac, C. P. made sure they stayed in Detroit long enough to see the Tigers play at Briggs Stadium. He had primed Arnie with tales of the great Hank Greenberg and Charlie Gehringer. By the time they took their seats in the stadium, Arnie was spouting the players' stats. He was drawn into the game and diligently kept a record of runs, hits and errors in his program.

Leaving Detroit and heading to New York, Arnie chatted incessantly about the game. C. P. regaled Arnie with tales of Joe DiMaggio battling Ted Williams for the American League MVP. Arnie was silent as his grandpa told him about the Iron Horse, Lou Gehrig, one of the best ever to play the game. By the time they walked into Yankee Stadium, Arnie's eyes were as big as catcher's mitts. The stadium seats were packed with fans who cheered each hit and defensive play. In Arnie's young mind something clicked. This was different than the baseball he had watched in the recreation leagues in Ogden. It was sport played at an entirely different level, and he liked it.

C. P. had been a baseball player in his younger years, and his interest in sports was focused on America's pastime. He didn't pay much attention to the relatively new game of basketball, but he showed proper enthusiasm for Arnie's success. Years earlier, Arnie had seen a glimmer of his own future when he watched his grandfather pitching in a local baseball game. Initially he had thought that his grandpa, then in his forties, was too old to be playing baseball, especially as a pitcher. C. P. pitched with his right arm for four innings and then, when his right arm became tired, switched to his left arm for the remainder of the game—without a noticeable change in speed or performance. This feat was notable to Arnie, not only because of the talk it generated among the fans watching the game, but also because it made him think that since his grandfather was a good athlete, perhaps he had some of that same magic running in his own veins.

In his early teens, Arnie often walked to the nearby elementary school hoping to find a pickup game or meet friends to play ball with. It was not uncommon for older kids to come to the playground looking for an easy game. It was also not uncommon for them to leave soundly beaten. It was easy to underestimate Arnie. He was tall and skinny, almost awkward, but his motor skills were quickly catching up with his height. It soon became apparent to these playground opponents that even at his relatively young age, Arnie was transformed once he got his hands on a basketball.

After being cut from the ninth-grade team, Arnie had all but forgotten about playing basketball at Central Junior High. He told himself that he wasn't bothered with the idea that his basketball career would never extend beyond his driveway court. Nonetheless, he sometimes found himself looking in the school gym watching the ninth- and tenth-grade teams practice, doing drills in sweat-drenched jerseys with their sneakers squeaking on the clean gym floor. He knew all of the players from his earlier unsuccessful attempt to make the team.

One day in mid-November he noticed that the man standing on the floor under the basket gently encouraging the players was not the same man who had dashed his dreams of junior high basketball stardom. Mr. Welch, the previous part-time basketball coach, had resigned his coaching position to pursue other interests. In fact, he had been so entrenched in those other interests at the beginning of the season that he hadn't put any thought into who would be on the team; he'd simply chosen the same players from the previous year's team. That was the real reason Arnie hadn't made the team. He didn't have time for any new players, even if, like Arnie, they were taller than himself by a good eight inches.

Mr. Welch's replacement was ninth- and tenth-grade physical education teacher Bill Kinner. This former consensus all-American basketball player from the University of Utah was a better all-around choice for coach. Not only did he bring real-world experience, but he also had what Mr. Welch lacked: a passion for basketball. He was six foot three inches tall, with jet black hair. His tall frame supported lean and sinewy muscles that had been carved from hours in the gym playing ball. At twenty-eight years of age, he looked like he could still compete with the best players of the day. His huge hands were partly responsible for his ability to make deadly accurate passes during his college career. In the classroom his dashing good looks made most tenth-grade girls wish they had a chance to win his heart. As a coach on the basketball court he was a gentleman. He commanded respect from his young players because that is what he gave them.

Arnie was in Bill Kinner's P.E. class and knew the teacher fairly well. On the day the students were practicing the game of basketball in class, Bill took note of how comfortable Arnie looked dribbling the ball. With a new interest in potential talent, Coach Kinner softly grabbed Arnie's elbow from behind as he stood in line to practice free throws. A firm voice said, "Arnie, why aren't you playing basketball for the team?" Arnie looked down an inch into the face of Coach Kinner and said, "I tried out but didn't make the cut."

Following a soft chuckle, Coach Kinner replied, "How can they expect us to win any games when all we have is a bunch of five-foot-ten-inch kids who can't jump or shoot? Then we have you, a totem pole walking around school and you're not even playing! If you can't do anything else, you'll get some rebounds. Be in the gym ready to go after school; you're on the team."

Arnie's shoes seemed nailed to the floor; his feet wouldn't move and he couldn't find the words to respond. He finally managed to utter a barely audible "okay." He raced home as soon as school was out and shouted the news as he bounced around the kitchen.

Following school the next day, Arnie reported to the gym and was assigned an old uniform that read "Central" across the front and "Cubs" across the back. Since the team had been working out for six weeks prior to him joining, the other team members had all of the new uniforms. His was well-worn, at least three years old, and the stitching behind the letters on his jersey had started to stretch with age, causing the capital "C" in "Central" to droop pitifully. Both the jersey and the shorts were tight, and he couldn't find any others in the pile of uniforms that were any bigger. As he stood up from the bench in the locker room, his new teammates couldn't help but wonder why Coach Kinner had recruited Ichabod Crane to join the team.

After a warm-up, Coach Kinner had the team scrimmage to see if the new kid would show some promise or bounce the ball off his foot and out of bounds. At first glance the boy appeared to fit his body as well as he fit into his uniform. To the coach's surprise, however, the first time Arnie was passed the ball he treated it like an old friend. He dribbled it twice, put the ball over his head and shot it with both hands from two feet beyond the top of the key. The only noise his defender heard was the sound of cords popping as the ball dropped straight through the net.

Arnie started every game the rest of the season. He was second on the team in scoring and led the team in rebounds. His defense was outstanding for a young man in his first experience with organized basketball. The Central Cubs finished second in the junior high league that year.

That summer he saw his father on a few occasions and even spent several long weekends with his dad and his new stepmom, Lu, on fishing trips to Cliff Lake, Montana. Arnie had learned the art of fly-fishing from his dad. Both he and Arn were adept at softly laying a dry fly on the surface of a lake or stream with only the slightest ripple on the water. Lu, however, was a rookie at the sport and would beat the water to a froth. She was a good sport and tried hard, but never learned the art. Her fly lines, leaders and tippets more commonly ended up tangled than not. Each occurrence brought a resolute but quiet "damn" from her lips. For Arnie, those few weekends spent beneath cerulean summer skies were all he could ask for—and never long enough.

It was a fact accepted by the coaches and players at Central that Arnie had already made the team when he showed up to report for the first day of basketball tryouts the next November. Even though his place on the team was assured, he hustled on every play, jumped high for every rebound and put fire on every pass during tryouts. He tried to bring the same hustle and hard work that he had seen in Yankee Stadium several years earlier to every play he made in that little gym.

Evidently Coach Kinner took note of his extra effort. On Friday afternoon of the week of tryouts, Arnie wanted to leave class just a little early. He knew that the team roster would be posted on the same gym door where he had been disappointed a year earlier. He raced down the hallway and stood in front of the glass-paneled door where the piece of paper was taped. Working his way through the crowd of twenty or so shorter kids he knew from tryouts, he felt slaps on his shoulder.

The team roster announcement began:

1941 CENTRAL B BALL TEAM
TEAM CAPTAIN: ARNIE FERRIN

He didn't even finish reading the list. He opened the doors of the gym where his teammates were waiting for him. The eleven players who had made the team walked out of the school together thinking that the other schools in their district had better watch out. Central Junior High had a big gun and his name was Arnie.

MAKING ENEMIES
OUT OF COUNTRYMEN

*A Jap's a Jap. I don't want any of them here. They are a dangerous element.
There is no way to determine their loyalty. . . . It makes no difference
whether he is an American citizen, he is still a Japanese. American citizen-
ship does not necessarily determine loyalty. . . . But we must worry about
the Japanese all the time until he is wiped off the map.*

— LIEUTENANT GENERAL
JOHN L. DEWITT,
ADMINISTRATOR OF THE JAPANESE
AMERICAN RELOCATION PROGRAM

Wat fiddled with the change in his pocket and
peered around the tall bodies that stood between him and the glass
store counter. He slowly marched forward in line until his turn came.
Pulling the list from his pocket, Wat started explaining his order, but
stopped short when the man in the white apron looked over his head
and asked the next person in line, "What can I getcha?" Wat might
as well have been invisible, and in a way he was, at least to the store
owner who chose to serve customers with a whiter skin tone first.

Only after there were no other patrons in line did the man allow Wat to place an order. This was not the first time Wat had been ignored because of his heritage, and it wouldn't be the last. Having grown up on a segregated street in segregated America, Wat was used to standing on one side of a store with other minorities while white customers received preferential treatment and passed him by.

In the 1930s and '40s, racism was commonplace in America. It would be decades before the civil rights movement would change the way Americans viewed and treated each other. World War II–era racism was not overt or always recognizable. Most people outwardly would have seemed patriotic and inoffensive, but at the core of many were degrading, fearful and hateful views and opinions based on intolerance, ignorance and prejudice. Words that would be considered racist and extremely offensive today were splashed across the front pages of newspapers on a daily basis, while racial epithets were spoken second-naturedly across kitchen tables throughout America. Propaganda posters in America portrayed the Japanese as subhuman: "Your enemy, the Jap"; "Don't talk, rats have big ears"; and "The Jap way, cold-blooded murder." The obscenely caricatured Tokyo Kid featured on propaganda posters had massive lips that curled around vampiric fangs dripping with drool. He always carried a bloodied dagger, presumably to stab you in the back, and spoke in rhyming broken English. Other posters showed mustachioed Japanese soldiers with squinty eyes and round glasses stealing away beautiful white-skinned women, as if the Japanese were bent on robbing Americans of their virtue. Popular songs with titles like "The Japs Haven't Got a Chinaman's Chance" and "You're a Sap, Mr. Jap" poured over the radio waves.

The prejudice against Wat and his family was twofold: they were looked down on for both their heritage and their poverty. Many of the businesses on 25th Street had separate facilities for anyone who wasn't white. This part of the city that Wat called home was the secret that everyone was aware of but refused to address. Most of the people who lived there were shunned by the rest of Ogden, who chose not to see the poverty that existed just a few blocks from their homes. This prejudice revealed the duplicity of the city: the whores and the winos were the ones who watched out for the youngsters of 25th Street—Samaritans who would give nickels to Wat's younger brothers for candy. Society had cast these people off and they had gathered here to survive, desperation having stripped them of any pretenses and prejudices.

Since he was a child, Wat had tried not to be noticed and spent most of his time too engaged in sports to get into trouble. On those occasions when Wat might have been tempted to act out or rebel, he quickly curtailed himself. Anything that might reflect poorly on him would have been viewed as a shameful act by his family and the local Japanese American community. All the Misaka children lived by a strict code of conduct that dictated they do nothing that was not honorable. Just like their parents had in Japan, Wat and his brothers understood that the Japanese culture would not stand for dishonorable children whose actions tarnished the family name with *haji,* or shame. For the Misakas, moral and academic excellence were responsibilities they bore in front of the community.

Unfortunately, that sense of honor was not always reciprocated. During the war, for example, GIs traveling through Ogden would make their way from the railroad depot up 25th Street, where Wat's younger brothers often played. At times they lashed out at the Japanese boys they saw on the street. Since the bombs had dropped on Pearl Harbor, the buffer that had separated Wat and his family from the prejudices of some of their fellow Americans had become thinner. Wat never felt that his life was in danger, but he realized that some people would choose to see race first rather than see him for who he was: just an average American kid who loved to shoot hoops and run the bases.

Following the raid by the Japanese military on U.S. naval forces at Pearl Harbor, many government and military officials believed the Japanese were planning a full-scale attack on the West Coast of the United States. The aggressive and decisive military victory by the Japanese in much of Asia further exacerbated fears that Emperor Hirohito's war machine was unstoppable.

Reeling from the heavy losses in the Pacific and in part due to public rage, President Franklin D. Roosevelt signed Executive Order 9066 on February 19, 1942, allowing local military commanders to designate areas within the United States as "exclusion zones," from which any person could be kept from entering or residing in. On May 3, 1942,

Civilian Exclusion Order No. 346 was issued, ordering all individuals of Japanese ancestry in exclusion zones encompassing all of California and most of Oregon and Washington to move to temporary "war relocation camps." There were no exclusion zones designated in Utah, and so the Misaka family was able to maintain some semblance of normal life on 25th Street in Ogden during the war.

To provide housing in isolated yet supervised areas, the U.S. government hastily erected twenty-seven internment camps scattered throughout California, Arizona, Colorado, Wyoming, Idaho, Utah and Arkansas. More than 120,000 Japanese Americans, two-thirds of whom were U.S. citizens and half of whom were children, were subjected to this mass relocation program. They were told to only take personal belongings they could carry on their backs. Because of the psychological turmoil they were suffering, most of the interned didn't have much time to sell their property. Many of their homes were simply abandoned.

The camps were erected on barren ground and surrounded with barbed-wire fences. Each camp was patrolled by armed guards. Residents could leave the camps only with special permission. The conditions at the camps were spartan at best. Housing consisted of tar-paper–covered barracks without plumbing or cooking areas, group bathrooms without partitions and cots for beds. Food costs were budgeted at forty-five cents per day per person. Maintaining private family lives in these overcrowded and public conditions was impossible.

The Central Utah Relocation Center was the fifth largest city in Utah while nearly 9,000 people of Japanese descent lived within its borders. The name of the camp was changed when those in charge realized that the abbreviated name of the camp could be pronounced "curse." The name "Delta" was proposed because of the close proximity to a nearby town of the same name, but the largely Mormon population of Delta objected to being associated with a "prison for the innocent." The final name of the camp, "Topaz," was inspired by a nearby mountain where topaz rock was found.

In the desolate Utah desert, detainees coerced the harsh land to sprout life. They tried to create a semblance of normalcy while surrounded by walls of desolation that stretched for hundreds of miles.

Over time, the people interred there gained the trust of those who ran the camp and were allowed to find work in neighboring towns.

Those in the camps showed remarkable tolerance for the hardships they were forced to endure. They knew that the only way for them to prove their loyalty to the country that doubted them was to submit themselves to their government's bidding. They didn't have the same political clout as the Germans or Italians, two immigrant groups that didn't face mass detention and were not classified as "enemy aliens" like the Japanese. This remarkable ability to deal with injustice is exemplified in the Japanese phrase *shikata ga nai,* meaning "nothing can be done about it." This oft-repeated statement meant more than just simple submission; it also represented an inner strength to persevere in the face of unbelievable treatment.

Wat wasted no time in transitioning from high school to college. He wasn't one to waffle over decisions or worry about their repercussions. He wanted to get on with his life and took the most reasonable path before him. There was no time to anguish over a career. He was good at math, so he would study engineering. His father's work ethic had worked its way into Wat's bones. He wanted a career that would provide him with opportunities that his father never found in his little barbershop.

But he couldn't go far from home. There were no scholarships waiting for him in spite of his athletic prowess, so he would have to continue to live at home and pay his own college expenses. The only option was for him to enroll at the local junior college, Weber College, and hope he could transfer to a larger school in a few years.

His intense focus allowed him a bit of shelter from what was going on in the world around him. While those Japanese Americans interred in the camps were separated from society because of racism, Wat was lucky enough to have walls around him that separated him from the prejudices of World War II–era America. He immersed himself in the relatively safe haven of college life.

His younger brother, Tats, was still in high school when the forced relocation began and wasn't so lucky. While the Misakas were not forced to move, they weren't immune from toxic encounters. At the same time Wat was burying his head in books, Tats was confronting racism face-first—sometimes with his fists.

There was no possibility of Wat's mother assisting him with college tuition; she had a hard enough time caring for her remaining two children. But Wat would not be dissuaded. He was like a train already on the way to its destination; nothing was going to stop him from getting the engineering education he wanted. To pay his college bill, Wat secured a position in the college gym, working in the same place he would spend his free time and endless hours of recreation. Saturdays were still spent at home assisting in the barbershop, while weekdays were filled with study, sports and work. His time was stretched so thin that there wasn't much left for things like dating and socializing. His studies came easily to him, but he still spent hour after hour studying, just as he spent hours playing whatever the seasonal sport was.

In the early 1940s, college basketball players didn't have the same singular focus that today's players have. Professional basketball hadn't yet been elevated to celebrity status and many of the professional players led inglorious lives. A shoe contract didn't mean tens of millions of dollars in ad campaigns as it does today; instead, it meant you got two pairs of Chuck Taylors a year. Players who succeeded in mentioning a cereal brand during an interview might be rewarded with a generous gift of a case of that cereal. Wat, like other college athletes at the time, didn't focus his entire life in pursuit of sports because there was little prospect of success. No false aspirations of a career in sports clouded his plans for the future, but he still wanted to excel, and practiced hard throughout the season.

Wat's drive for athletic excellence was inspired by his own expectations of himself and also a desire to outdo his longtime friend, George Shimizu. Both of them lived in downtown Ogden and shared a common bond of ethnicity. George was a few years older than Wat and inspired him to get involved in a myriad of sports. George played basketball and lettered in tennis in high school; Wat lettered in basketball and track. After high school, Wat followed George to Weber College. Wat seemed to have magic hands. Whatever he picked up instantly became an extension of himself, even a table tennis paddle. While at Weber College, Wat even managed to squeeze some time in for a city league tennis tournament, where he played doubles with George.

By today's sports standards, Wat was almost Lilliputian at five foot seven—and even in the early 1940s he was considered somewhat short for basketball, even though during his college years it was rare to see a player taller than six foot two. Bob Peterson, a local high school player, was often called "Giant Peterson" in the papers even though he was only six foot one. Prevalent wisdom taught that the taller you were, the slower you were. It wasn't until Bob Kurland and George Mikan proved the basketball world wrong in the mid-1940s that people accepted that basketball players could be tall, quick and athletic. On defense, Wat was maniacal and relentless. He had a limitless supply of energy, and if he ever got tired on the court, his opponents never would have known it by the way he tracked them like a shadow.

In everyday life Wat's posture was straight and he carried his head high. Once he donned his basketball uniform and stepped onto the court, his shoulders tightened and his legs arched like springboards. His whole body leaned forward toward the action with his arms extended, looking like he was ready to pounce on his opponents. Wat was pure kinetic energy every minute he was on the floor. On defense he pushed beyond his short stature to take on typically taller players, and yet he often got the better of those matchups. His offensive play was just as spirited.

Something about basketball was different than the other sports Wat played. The difference wasn't in the way he played the game—he approached most everything in his life seriously and with passion—but in the way he was recognized for his ability. Spectators at the Weber College track meets Wat participated in came and went, as whatever drama there was in tabulating the winners and losers quietly went on behind the scenes. Basketball, however, is a game designed for an audience: it's an epic drama that plays itself out in real time. There are heroes and villains, underdogs and hegemons. The spectators' shouts, cheers, catcalls and intensity somehow imbue the players with additional strength. Ogdenites loved to watch basketball, as was shown by the frequency that traveling and exhibition teams came through town. Wat's ability to overcome his short stature with skill and determination made him a crowd favorite and secured him a place on the Weber College team alongside his high school teammate, Max Jensen.

Weber College was one of six teams in the Intermountain Junior College Conference that stretched from southern Utah to Idaho, and included teams in Idaho, Utah, and Colorado. Wartime gasoline rationing and restrictions against buses being used to transport college sports teams made scheduling games difficult. Some college squads had dissolved due to the lack of available opponents and players lost to the ranks of the armed forces. Weber College was lucky to be a member of a viable league, and there were several service teams at nearby Hill Field and Defense Depot Ogden stocked with postgraduate enlisted men that the college team could scrimmage against. To stir up interest, Coach Reed Swenson even arranged for his team to play traveling exhibition teams such as the Clowns, St. Louis Ghosts and Abe Saperstein's Harlem Globetrotters, which were consistently beating the best college teams in the country—and on one occasion even the Minneapolis Lakers. It was common for a team like the Ghosts to come to town and play several teams in one night, beating them all. On one occasion, the independent Ogden Pioneers agreed to play against the St. Louis team with altered rules that allowed a player unlimited fouls and no fear of being ejected from play. Four referees were needed to officiate the game. Even the large church leagues in Ogden got in on the action, but never mounted much of a challenge against their professional guests.

To keep his squad playing, Reed loaded his players into his Plymouth and drove sometimes hundreds of miles to meet opposing teams. Six players, plus the coach, were crammed together like sardines in a can with swooping fenders. Wat, being the smallest on the team, was always up front next to the coach, who drove their cramped chariot at a brisk sixty miles an hour with one sprawling hand on the center of the steering wheel. An endless tune reverberated from his lips as his other hand was busy playing with his large nose and bushy eyebrows. Once they reached their destination, it was not unlike watching a clown car in a circus unload. But instead of happy clowns with painted faces, they were tall, sleepy basketball players with sore backs.

Coach Swenson was friendly but didn't talk much during the long trips, and didn't say much anywhere else for that matter. When he *was* talking he was probably saying "drive the ball," his favorite offensive philosophy. Basketball in the West was still not advanced, but Reed did teach his squad to play a simple offensive style he called the "figure eight."

By the close of the 1942 season, the Weber College team had clinched the conference title. During one of the final games, Wat scored more than twenty points, almost half the team's total. He was chosen the team's MVP that season. Another MVP award was given to Wat for his performance in the Intermountain Nisei League Tournament, featuring teams from independent Japanese leagues based as far away as Los Angeles. He was named MVP of the tournament in spite of his team taking second place after losing in the final game to the perennial champions, the Golden Nippons of Salt Lake City. Coach Swenson rewarded Wat's effort that year by naming him, along with Max Jensen, as co-captain for his sophomore year.

Wat had found a niche where he could succeed in his endeavors. He was content to enjoy his life and not worry about the political and social problems around him. Because Utah was not one of the areas that had been a target of the relocation program, Wat was free to do as he wanted.

Years after spending time together as boys skiing on the makeshift slopes east of Ogden, Roy Yoshioka and Wat had ended up on opposite ends of life. Wat's relative success at Weber College was in stark contrast to the life that Roy was living. During their senior year at Ogden High, Roy's family moved to Los Angeles. They kept in touch, and when Roy's family was forced from their home and taken to a camp in Arizona, he detailed his fears in letters to Wat. It was one of the few times Wat let anything get in the way of his studies. He couldn't help but think of his friend trapped in a sweltering desert camp while he pursued a college education. He felt helpless—one man against an entire system—but he was determined to help.

For those in the camps, pursuing a college education was one of the ways they could leave. Roy sent Wat a letter, begging him to find someone to fill out the required paperwork and make the necessary arrangements for his release. This was no small favor. Whoever wrote the letters would be vouching for Roy's character, not to mention guaranteeing him an education, a steady job or both. Most of the people Wat knew were Japanese, and thus ineligible to sponsor Roy. So Wat looked to his teammates. The father of teammate John Dixon happened to be the president of Weber College, Henry Aldous Dixon. Wat couldn't have found a better person to vouch for Roy's character than President Dixon. He was well known and respected, and was warm and kind to his students. Later in life he became president of Utah State Agricultural College, and eventually he was elected to the U.S. House of Representatives. When Wat came to him about helping his childhood friend, Dr. Dixon didn't hesitate to offer his help and arranged to get Roy a position working alongside Wat in the college gym.

At first glance, it would appear that Arnie's and Wat's lives growing up in the same town were so different that they might as well have occurred on different continents. Somehow—even though they walked the same halls at Ogden High and played on the same basketball court just a few years apart—they had never crossed paths.

Arnie's father was relatively wealthy, while Wat's family never overcame their poverty. Somehow Wat had succeeded in preventing the foul atmosphere of downtown Ogden from staining his outlook on life, while Arnie had never been exposed to such situations, living on the other end of town in a comfortable house in a quiet neighborhood. Wat was never aware that he had been deprived of little luxuries like an official basketball hoop and a double-wide driveway. But he was rich in ways that Arnie had longed for as an only child raised primarily by his grandparents. Wat's mother was a loving woman who supported and encouraged him, and he had two brothers to wrestle with and watch over.

Arnie isolated himself from those closest to him, while Wat isolated himself from the influences outside the walls of his home.

Though their lives were different in many ways, the grief of losing a parent was something that molded them similarly in their early years, quickly aging them beyond youthful bliss. Death leaves empty hearts and questions that are simply unanswerable to a young boy.

The disparity of their lives ceased when, in an odd twist, their lives intersected on the sports page of the local newspaper. They were both front-page news, separated by only a few columns: Arnie at Ogden High, Wat at Weber College. They both had basketball, and it was basketball that would finally bring them together.

GROWING PAINS

You can't win unless you learn how to lose.

— KAREEM ABDUL-JABBAR

The sterile smell of the doctor's office was almost worse than the pain in Arnie's knee. The fatherly looking doctor pushed on his swollen knee, applying gentle pressure to stress the joint.

"You have injured the cartilage on the inside of your knee. If we're lucky, you'll be on crutches for two or three weeks. If we aren't lucky, you'll need surgery to repair the damage."

Knowing it wouldn't do any good, Arnie still pleaded with the doctor to let him play in the championship game on Thursday. Without him, his team stood little chance in the final game against their crosstown rival Lewis Junior High. From under his bushy gray eyebrows the doctor looked at Arnie, firmly said no, and left to see his next patient. Arnie was left to be nothing but a witness to the chaos that followed for his team; he was helpless to assist.

The coach didn't give Arnie the lecture he was expecting, but neither he nor the rest of his teammates could hide the disappointment that was painted on their faces when Arnie hobbled into the gym for practice. Coach Kinner couldn't blame the kid. Arnie was still awkward and had a habit of overcompensating for his lack of social graces. And like most boys his age, his mind went into neutral whenever cheerleaders were around.

The preceding Friday, after the buzzer ending the final game of the regular season, a cheerleader named Charlene Sowers sauntered across the court to Arnie and invited him to go skiing with her family the next day. He didn't even think of the championship game. The impassioned warnings Coach Kinner had repeated throughout the season admonishing his team to avoid any activity that might cause injury were far from his mind as he stared at Charlene's bright smile and curly hair. He had never been on a date before and he was just realizing that this newfound acceptance was an unintended consequence of his success on the team.

After the game, he spent almost as much time talking about his upcoming date as he did about the victory. Chatting with his friends in the locker room, Arnie didn't understand why his teammates were worried about him skiing the weekend before the big game. All he could think of was sharing hot chocolate with the cutest girl on the cheer squad. "Besides," he told his friends, "I've been skiing a couple of times before."

The doe-eyed couple were among the first in line at the rope tow Saturday morning at Snowbasin, the new ski resort in the mountain valley above Ogden. The subzero temperatures the night before had caked a layer of snow and ice along the rope tow. After waiting his turn in the short line, Arnie grabbed the rope with his wet gloves and held on as it jerked up the hill. He was halfway to the top when he realized his soggy glove was frozen to the icy rope. He had a horrible vision of being pulled into the motor-driven pulley and began to shake like a helpless fish on a frozen hook. As he neared the top of the hill he panicked, and in a frantic attempt to free himself he lost his balance. The edge of his ski dug into the snow and jerked his leg to the side.

As he fell he felt something subtle in his knee. It wasn't necessarily painful; it was a feeling more like gears that didn't quite fit together. He was dragged twenty feet to the end of the tow before his hand slipped out of his glove. His first thought was of his wounded pride; he had created quite a spectacle. His knee had been twisted badly when his ski bindings hadn't released. As he tried to push himself up on the slippery slope and put weight on his skis, the searing pain began.

Not only was it a terribly short first date, but it would turn out to be a disaster for the Central Junior High Cubs basketball team.

The crammed gymnasium was filled with 1,500 teenagers from Central and rival Lewis Junior High, and the air was hot and thick. Most of the crowd was shouting encouragement at their respective teams as they warmed up on the floor. Giddy cheerleaders bounced along the court trying fruitlessly to organize the boisterous students into a cohesive group that could all shout the same cheer or sing the same song. They were being all but ignored by the young fans who just wanted to yell.

Feeling some responsibility for Arnie's injured knee, Charlene had not taken her usual spot on the floor with the cheerleaders. Instead, she was sitting on the end of the team bench next to Arnie, who was dressed in a white shirt and tie instead of his basketball uniform. He felt terrible; the heart of the team was ambulatory only if he used his crutches. To feel involved somehow, he shouted encouragement to his teammates as they warmed up. He replayed the events on the slopes of Snowbasin over and over in his mind, as if he could change what happened by analyzing it. Or maybe, he thought, if he prayed hard enough he could change the unforgivable reality of his compromised knee. Each time he thought of it, he wished away that snowy morning on the slopes.

After another round of encouragement, Charlene pranced off to take her place with the other cheerleaders in the out-of-bounds area under the basket.

Huddling around Coach Kinner in front of the bench, the team listened to his encouraging words. Arnie stood behind the able-bodied players, hoping his role on the team had been overstated. As the starting five took the floor for the start of the game, Arnie slid to the end of the bench to allow the other players to sit closer to the coach. When the players took their places on the floor, all Arnie could do was hope for some miracle that would elevate the play of his teammates and allow a different outcome of the game than he was expecting.

The first play of the game set the tone for the rest of the evening.

After controlling the jump, Lewis's speedy guard slashed to the basket and gently laid the ball off the backboard and into the hoop. It was immediately apparent that the Central Cubs were badly overmatched without Arnie in the game to provide leadership, shoot the ball and rebound. In spite of determined play by Central, the final outcome of the game was never in doubt, so both coaches played their second-stringers for most of the fourth quarter. For the Central fans, the game couldn't end quickly enough. The final score was 39–18 in favor of Lewis.

What started out as a cheering competition between the two schools' fans had died down as the game wore on, with the remaining Central supporters sitting quietly in their assigned section of the gym. Most of them had left in the fourth quarter, before they had to witness the hopes of a league championship dashed on the hardwood floor. When the referee finally blew his whistle ending the painfully long game, the Central bleachers were vacant except for the parents of a few players, the principal, some of the teachers and a few die-hard students.

Arnie hobbled after the team into the locker room. Partial responsibility for the thrashing weighed heavily on his slender shoulders. None of the team felt like going out to celebrate as they had planned earlier that evening. The disappointing loss had robbed them of any desire to be together. Mostly they all just wanted to go home and forget the game. Arnie got a ride home, and as he walked in the door on his crutches he smelled hot chocolate and cookies, Ida's specialty—a soothing balm for his heavy heart.

Arnie spent the summer before the eleventh grade idly as his knee healed. Most of the time the knee didn't bother him, but occasionally he felt a sharp pain and catching along the inside of the joint. But it was not enough to deter his anticipation of the upcoming basketball season. He continued to see Charlene on occasion, but spent more time with his friends and teammates. As incoming juniors at Ogden High School, the prospects of change were both exciting and frightening.

Ogden High was the newest high school in Utah in 1941. It was financed through the Works Progress Administration, a New Deal program created by President Roosevelt in 1935, and the building was completed in 1937. The school still stands on the east side of Harrison Boulevard, a perfect tribute to the art deco style of design. It boasted the most ornate auditorium in the state and one of the most beautiful in the western United States. The interior of the school was replete with aluminum chandeliers and fixtures, while exterior doors were adorned with simple geometric lines. The hallways had walls faced with matched segments of imported Italian marble. Stylized sunbursts were found over doorways, above the auditorium stage, at hallway intersections and inlaid in the floor. A full palette of art deco colors, ranging from Chinese green to pink and vermilion, graced even the common areas of the school. Architectural details were finished with gold leaf, and only the best woods were used for doors, casings and seats in the auditorium. Though much smaller in scale, Ogden High School looked as though it came from the same lineage as the Empire State and Chrysler buildings in New York City.

The school loomed like a castle above the small homes that surrounded it, a massive temple in honor of decorative modernism. This monument to education was built for the ages and had a price tag of $1 million dollars—the first school west of the Mississippi to cost as much. Most importantly for Arnie, it had the best basketball gym in the state. While many schools had a three-quarter-size court with two backcourt lines, Ogden High had a full-size playing surface with a well-constructed and finely finished hardwood floor. As Arnie entered the gym for the first time, he remembered the mysterious aura that filled Yankee Stadium three years earlier as the players in pinstripes trotted onto the field. He pictured himself trotting onto the court in an Ogden Tiger uniform, and hoped that this gym in some way would generate the same feeling.

In the fall of 1941, Coach Aaron Horne didn't hold formal tryouts for the Ogden High basketball team. Instead he invited those players he wanted on the team to drop by the office and pick up their uniforms. The returning senior starters on the team had seen the incoming juniors play in junior high. Arnie's reputation preceded him; he was immediately assigned to the starting five. Anticipation was high for Ogden High's upcoming season, with talk of possible league and state championships. Coach Horne didn't have the extensive basketball knowledge of Central Junior High's Coach Kinner. He was foremost a teacher, and his role as the head of the basketball team took a distant second to his other work responsibilities. He believed in hard work, hustle and a pressure defense, and hoped the offense would somehow take care of itself.

By December the team was busy with practices and scrimmages. Around Ogden, trees sparkled with lights, and tinsel and ornaments filled the living rooms of homes. Families were busy planning their Christmas parties and Arnie was looking forward to a break from school. On Sunday afternoon, December 7, Arnie was in the kitchen of Charlene Sowers home having dinner with her family. Charlene was the first to hear the rapid pounding on the door.

She greeted Ott Bramwell, Arnie's best friend and teammate, who rushed wide-eyed into the kitchen to tell everyone the news. The radio was tuned to the CBS broadcast of *The World Today,* and like millions around the world they listened raptly to the report on the surprise attack by the Japanese against unprepared U.S. forces at Pearl Harbor. Immediately following the report, as if in an attempt to buoy the spirits of an American public angered by the tragic events of the morning, the network played the number one song in the country at the time, Glenn Miller's "Chattanooga Choo Choo."

All young men who attended Ogden High were, by district mandate, required to enroll in the Junior Reserve Officers' Training Corps program for two years. The JROTC class was, in essence, military training for high school students. One day per week students were required to wear army uniforms, stand for inspection and drill. Classes were taught in military theory and cadets enjoyed the shooting range, even though they used .22 caliber rifles instead of the M1s used by the military. Arnie excelled in JROTC and entertained thoughts of enlisting in the Air Force following his senior year. For the time being, however, his focus was far from the war.

Following six weeks of intense practice and a preseason schedule of games, Ogden was ready to begin league play on January 2, 1942. The sportswriters for the local newspaper touted the Tigers as one of the favorites to win the league championship, with three excellent new players—including Arnie, who even as an eleventh-grader was close to being a sensation in his hometown.

An hour before the first game was scheduled to begin, Arnie was intercepted entering the locker room by Coach Horne and a member of the school administration. They had some bad news for him. With anticipation of the looming Christmas vacation, Arnie had forgotten to make up a test he had missed, and as a result he was deemed ineligible to play. Ogden High would play their rival, Weber High, without him. This was only the second time in his young basketball career that he spent the game on the bench. The Tigers played well, but without Arnie in the lineup they weren't good enough. Ogden lost at home to Weber, 31–28. Coach Horne came up to Arnie in the locker room after the game, placed his hand on his star's shoulder and stated, "We need you, Arnie." He got the message and took the test the following Monday in order to regain his eligibility.

Ogden lost their second game of the season to Logan High before their fortunes turned and they started to perform like the preseason favorites they were. They finished league play with a record of 7–4, which was good enough to qualify for the state tournament. Led by Arnie's team-high scoring, the Tigers started the tournament by defeating Carbon High School, but lost in the second round to Provo High. It wasn't much of a season, and followed an unfortunate trend that Arnie was beginning to see in his life. Nonetheless, his indomitable spirit kept him looking forward to his senior year.

Knowing that Ida and C. P. were aging and that Arnie needed transportation, Arn bought his son a lumbering 1939 brown Plymouth four-door sedan during his junior year, which was presented to him when he received his driver's license. Being one of only two students at Ogden High to own a car, Arnie's popularity increased exponentially. Every day after school his car was draped with anxious friends. Friday and Saturday evenings they loaded into the sedan and headed to the White City Ballroom to dance to the music of Jimmy Dorsey and Benny Goodman. But in spite of a large group of close friends and his star basketball status, sadness continued to stand in the wings of Arnie's life.

By the fall of Arnie's senior year, C. P.'s health was failing. He had worked hard his entire life, and now some injuries from an earlier automobile accident were catching up with him. The rest of the family knew the end was near. He was sixty-eight years old and spent most of his time at home, cared for by Ida. C. P. was the closest thing Arnie had ever had to a father. Seeing his grandfather in such a state was heartbreaking, but he bore it like he did all setbacks: he wore a smile and played on.

On Wednesday, December 23, with school having just ended for the Christmas holiday, preparations were being made throughout the city to celebrate the season. Snow drifted softly from dark gray skies and laid in fluffy piles on the side of the roads and sidewalks. Families everywhere were fixing food and tending to last-minute shopping. Arn, Lu, Ida and Arnie, however, were at the Ferrin home, gathered around C. P.'s bed. They tenderly held his hands and stayed with him as he took his last breath.

A sense of emptiness filled Arnie, a numbness that left him void of emotion. Perhaps it was the innocence of youth that allowed him to deny the significance of his loss. Perhaps it was that human characteristic that can be found in everyone that allowed him to build emotional walls that held out the pain when it became too much to bear. Arnie relied on the few constants in his life as Christmas came and went. He coped the best way he knew how: he played ball.

Moe Moesinger had returned as basketball coach at Ogden High after having taken a one-year leave of absence. He took over a team that was considered the best in the state by most ardent basketball followers.

The first game of the season was a road game against rival Weber High, which Ogden High narrowly won in overtime. Arnie, as expected, led all scorers with sixteen points. Like grains of salt packed in a shaker, the team filled Arnie's sedan following the game for the trip back home. Transportation to and from road games was restricted due to wartime gasoline and rubber rationing. School districts were only allowed limited use of school buses. Personal cars were generally the only means of transportation. Each automobile owner was allowed to purchase three to five gallons of gas per week for nonessential purposes; essential uses allowed the owner to purchase greater amounts. Doctors, nurses, farmers and those charged with public safety could generally purchase all they needed. Fortunately for Arnie and the team, Arnie's father had put his twenty-acre estate in southern Ogden to good use: he developed the land and started a dairy. The Edgehill Dairy was allowed to purchase large quantities of gas for farm equipment, so when Arnie had burned through his three-gallon allotment, he drove to the dairy and filled up his tank. With a seemingly unlimited supply of fuel, Arnie's sedan became the team bus.

Other victories came one after another, with the margin of victory generally in double digits. Only a 37–34 road loss to South Cache, when Arnie was sidelined with a shoulder injury, spoiled an undefeated season of league play for the Tigers. The team looked forward to beginning the state tournament. They felt that winning the state championship was a goal that was finally within reach.

The day after their final regular season game, Coach Moesinger walked into the locker room before practice as the players donned their shorts and jerseys. He gathered his team around him and hung his head as he told them of the phone call he had just received. State officials had informed him that the state tournament had been canceled. School districts had been placed on strict rationing for the war effort, and transportation to Salt Lake City for the tournament games was a luxury they couldn't justify. There would be no state champion in 1943. Initially the boys thought the coach was joking, but the stern expression on his face quickly convinced them otherwise. The Tigers wouldn't have the chance to prove what those who followed Utah high school sports already knew: that Ogden High was, without a doubt, the best team in the state. Though it seemed insignificant in comparison to the team's disappointment, Arnie was named to the all-region and all-state teams for the second year in a row.

Before graduation, Arnie had been offered a basketball scholarship at Brigham Young University, eighty miles to the south. Tuition was $25 per quarter; however, driving back and forth between Provo and Ogden on weekends would require a larger investment in gas than the value of his scholarship. He considered attending the University of Utah, but he had not been recruited to play basketball for them. In the end, Arnie followed his sense of duty, along with some coaxing from friends, and decided to enlist in the Air Force.

He reported for his preinduction physical examination with medical records in hand, and met every requirement for enlistment until the last part of the physical: an orthopedic exam. After reviewing his records, the military doctor asked him to lie on the exam table. He took Arnie's left knee in his hands and applied firm pressure and a twist to the joint. The knee immediately locked and he was unable to straighten his leg. Arnie's application to the Air Force was summarily rejected. He tried enlisting in two other branches of the military with the same results. He could beat most opponents down a basketball floor and lay the ball against the backboard and into the hoop without much of a problem, but his knee wasn't good enough to allow him to defend his country.

It was a spring day in 1943, and Arnie sat on the floor in his room next to the bed and considered the hand that life had dealt him. He had never been one to wallow in disappointment, but that day he wallowed. He was seventeen and a half. His father had a separate life, he felt like a burden to his grandma and the armed services wouldn't take him.

Perhaps it was providence smiling down on a young man who had suffered some tough breaks in his life. Maybe it was just dumb luck. On the last day of school, Arnie walked out of Ogden High with a folded letter in his shirt pocket. The letter from Mr. David Peterson, the vice principal at the high school, was addressed to his brother, Vadal, head basketball coach at the University of Utah. The letter began, "Dear Vadal, I am pleased to introduce Arnie Ferrin . . ."

A UTAH MAN

We're up to snuff, we never bluff, we're game for any fuss.
No other gang of college men dare meet us in a muss.
So fill your lungs and sing it out and shout it to the sky,
We'll fight for dear old crimson for a Utah Man am I!
Ki-yi!

— University of Utah fight song

"Eggheads!"

Vadal spat the word out of his mouth like it was spoiled milk, making it sound like the foulest of obscenities.

"Every last one of them, eggheads!" the coach muttered to the empty hallway as he walked away from the list he had hung on the bulletin board a few days earlier. Ten or twelve names were scrawled on the typed note where he had requested that any student interested in playing basketball sign their name, list their area of study and attend the first practice of the season in early October, which was now just a few days away. All but two or three of the students who had signed the list were premed or engineering students. He had no delusions of championships. He just hoped to entice a few players to try out who could dribble and shoot the ball well enough to put a team on the court. Even that may have been asking too much.

"Maybe I can recruit the chess club," he thought as he turned on the lights in the girl's gym. Not finding the inspiration he was looking for, he shut the lights off again and turned back toward his makeshift office.

The overstuffed clipboard clattered on the desktop, sending tiny clouds of dust billowing around the hot metal lampshade. The air was thick and warm in the tiny office, which seemed to be nothing more than several closets bunched together. Illuminated solely by the small desktop lamp, the walls and shelves were heavily adorned with awards, trophies and overflowing boxes that had no place to be un-packed—all hinting at Coach Peterson's stellar seventeen-year career at the University of Utah.

His wooden chair squawked a short protest as Vadal seated him-self behind the desk and rested his head on one fist. He was used to success. As head coach of the Runnin' Redskins, Vadal had amassed a glittering record of 225 wins and 145 losses. As the coach of LDS High School in Salt Lake City prior to coming to the university, his team had won the consolation bracket of the 1926 High School National Championship Tournament.

This year was bucking the trend. Just thinking about the upcoming season gave Vadal a case of heartburn. Patching together a team would be challenging enough with only one returning player, but rumors had reached the cramped office that the other teams in the state were dis-banding. The Skyline Conference was going to curl up and die a piti-ful, whimpering death, leaving Vadal a man with a fight to win and no one to punch.

He was allergic to idleness and filled with a frenetic work ethic. The idea of packing it up for a season made as much sense as chopping off his own hand. He would have a team to coach even if he had to stock it with cheerleaders.

The insatiable drive that gave Vadal his reputation was born with him in Huntsville, Utah. One of nine sons born to Annie and Lars Peterson, Vadal and his brothers were raised on the family ranch, where each of them learned the meaning of hard work as they carried out endless chores. They were up early even in winter, when temperatures would plummet to twenty degrees below zero or lower.

The importance of education and giving one's best effort were principles the elder Petersons instilled in the souls of their children, and they lived as good examples of the values they espoused.

Each of the nine children became gifted athletes and starred in several sports at different colleges throughout Utah. Vadal was an all-conference end on the University of Utah football team and starting guard on the basketball team. He played catcher, and occasionally pitcher, on the baseball team, which he also captained. Vadal's older brother Ed was also a multisport athlete at both the University of Utah and Brigham Young University. He gained the nickname of the "Terrible Swede" for refusing to wear a helmet while earning all-conference football honors at Utah.

Vadal approached his coaching responsibilities with the same intensity he learned growing up in Ogden Valley, where he competed with his eight brothers on a daily basis. He demanded the same dedication from the athletes he coached. If you didn't work on the farm, you would starve. In his eyes, the same was true for basketball; if you didn't work hard enough, you would suffer and die a slow death—but even worse, in front of thousands of witnesses. Stress was part and parcel of coaching even when circumstances were favorable, and Vadal was no stranger to difficult times, on or off the court. The fall of 1943 was different; its challenges were uniquely exquisite.

The University of Utah's commitment to their athletic programs continued in spite of wartime restrictions. They were determined to put a competitive basketball team on the court no matter the difficulties. However, all of the senior players had been lost to the draft, leaving mostly incoming freshmen. The first-year students had to be either premed, predental or engineering students (all of whom could postpone military enlistment until after college), or those who were ineligible to enlist because of health issues. Neither category seemed ideally suited for finding quality athletes. Vadal had only one scholarship to offer, so the rest of the players would have to pay for tuition, books and fees—meaning most of them would have to pay to play basketball. Like rubbing salt in an already raw wound, Vadal didn't even have shoes or jockstraps to offer his athletes, because rubber was rationed during the war. If anyone wanted to play, he would have to provide his own equipment.

Even the university's athletic facilities were hard-hit during wartime. The Einar Nielson Field House, where the team planned to practice and play home games, was requisitioned and turned into barracks after the 1943 season when the military found it was in need of additional space to house its increasing numbers. The displaced Utes had to hunt for a new home court and coach's office. Vadal's office had been relocated to a nondescript building that housed a dance floor and a small women's basketball court. It would do for practices but was utterly unsuitable for games. Vadal had no option but to negotiate an agreement that allowed the team to play some of its home games in a small church-owned gym in downtown Salt Lake.

The Utes were one of seven teams in the Skyline Conference, created in 1938 when the seven charter schools resigned from the Rocky Mountain Athletic Conference. Less than ten years later the new conference had stopped operation because of gas and travel restrictions imposed by the government. It was hard to justify giving tires and gas to college athletes when there was a war going on.

Without conference foes to schedule games with, Vadal had few options. They would have to play games against any opponent he could find, but finding enough of them to fill a full season's schedule was another matter entirely. Most of the best college players in the nation were upperclassmen who had been drafted into military service and were now stationed at military bases scattered throughout the country. Luckily there were a number of bases throughout the West that sponsored basketball teams, most of which had two or three excellent varsity college players on the roster. Some even boasted professional players from the National Basketball League. The team from Fort Warren, Wyoming, included members of the Harlem Globetrotters. A game with them would be suicide.

The Utes weren't allowed to play independent or service teams according to the rules of their conference. That made no sense whatsoever to Vadal, since there were no other teams left in the conference to play. But if Vadal wanted a shot at any postseason tournaments he would have to abide by the rules. Brigham Young University, the Utes' rival to the south, had taken a trip earlier that season to play a series of nonconference games at Madison Square Garden against East Coast teams from Long Island University and Albright College. Since then,

Vadal had dreamed of taking his team to New York and playing on the Garden floor. However, looking at his current prospects and the fact that BYU had won only one of their games while in New York, maybe it was best to put any high hopes in cold storage.

Vadal had to choose between painful and ugly. If he abandoned the conference rules, the team could schedule a full slate of games against service and semipro teams. It would be a masochist's schedule, with the Utes pitted against some of the best basketball talent in the country—at any level. If he *did* follow conference rules it would still be ugly—but at least it wouldn't last long. There were only a handful of college teams who had announced plans to dress a full squad.

Nursing this young team was going to be a full-time burden even without having to worry about filling out the team's dance card. Looking for a way to spread around his misery and migraines, Vadal hired a graduate assistant named Keith Brown to function as the business manager for the team. Keith came with a strong recommendation that claimed he had a passion for detail and would follow any task to completion and beyond. Just the man for the job—someone who didn't understand the meaning of the word *impossible.* Keith's first assignment was a baptism by fire. His job was to do anything necessary, including begging, to find suitable teams to play. Without in-state rivals to compete against, the loss of local fan support and poor game attendance was a constant specter.

Vadal had chosen the right man for the job: Keith was relentless in his search. But even as tryouts began, there were only a handful of scheduled games on Vadal's calendar. Opposing teams' names were scrawled in big red letters through the end of November and early December. A junior college and several squads of military students at the university would start off the schedule. But January was dauntingly colorless, and February and March were completely blank.

Vadal leaned back in his chair and let out an exasperated sigh. He couldn't help but think of the 1927 New York Yankees feared "Murderers' Row" team. He chuckled and thought to himself, "the Pittsburgh Pirates had a better chance against the 1927 Yankees than we have of beating anybody." Any opponent would be the Row, and Vadal knew that his team, whomever they ended up being, was going to get murdered on the court.

In most years there would have been at least a handful of return-ing players on the team. This year there was only one: Fred Sheffield, a sophomore with springs for legs, who was a premed student with a draft exemption. Since he was the only player with previous major college experience, he would be captain by default. Other than that, Vadal would have to take whomever walked into the gym—as long as he came in his own sneakers.

A quiet knock sounded from the doorway of the office and Vadal looked up to see a nervous-looking student staring back at him.

"Can you tell me where I can find Coach Peterson?" the student asked.

"Right here," Vadal replied sourly. The coach lacked the buffer that exists for most people: whatever popped into his brain would fly im-mediately out of his mouth. What he lacked in discretion, he made up for with sarcasm.

In the dim light of the small office, all Arnie saw was a granite chin and two bulging eyes peering at him from under a brow that looked like a brick wall. An awkward pause forced Arnie to wonder if he was sup-posed to enter the office or wait for an invitation. The middle-aged man at the desk dipped his chin and raised a brow in an unspoken, "What do you want?"

Arnie patted his shirt pocket to make sure the letter of introduc-tion from Dave Peterson was where he had placed it a few hours earlier. He grabbed the envelope and ducked through the doorway. He leaned forward, stretching his long arm out to the desk, dropped the letter and snapped back to his position in the hallway.

"I'd like to try out for the basketball team," he said.

In what was probably the longest sentence he had used all day, Vadal responded, "Check the notice on the bulletin board and sign your name," then turned his attention to the newspaper on his desk. Arnie looked down at his letter feeling disappointed the coach hadn't even bothered to look at who it was from.

After suffering through another painful moment of silence, Arnie understood that the conversation was over and so turned and headed down the hall. He had taken only a few steps when he heard the coach shouting from his office, "Do you have your own shoes?"

Taking a few steps back, Arnie stretched his neck to look into the office again. "What?" he asked.

Without raising his eyes from his newspaper, Vadal explained, "You can try out if you have your own shoes!"

Still unsure of himself, Arnie silently shrugged his shoulders and walked down the hall to read the notice and sign his name. He scrawled his signature on the paper pinned to the soft cork bulletin board, listed his year in school as "freshman" and his major as "business." All the other players listed majors in engineering or medicine. All were freshman except two; one was a sophomore, the other a junior with a name he couldn't pronounce: Wataru Misaka.

With the skinny nuisance gone, Vadal reread a newspaper article highlighting the local church basketball leagues. It was as good a place to start as any, he supposed, as he picked up the phone to start his recruiting—if you could call it that. He considered it more of an earnest request to play for his team.

Tall and skinny, Herb Wilkinson could have been mistaken for a plump broomstick. Herb was in his family's kitchen when an unexpected phone call would ultimately set up one of the most decisive moments of his life.

He had received the call while helping his mother prepare dinner for their family of nine. It was a daily ritual that took hours, but it was a labor that she loved. Her husband was a physician who did well enough so that she didn't have to work out of their home to help meet the expenses of their large family. Gathering around the kitchen table for the evening meal and sharing stories of the day's events was still a daily tradition. Even though many of her children were old enough to have other interests, they all cherished their family dinners.

In his short life, Herb had bounced around Utah from the small town of Hurricane, where he was born, to Cedar City and then to Salt Lake City, where his father had settled down with his practice and begun experimenting with electrotherapy. He quickly gained a reputation as a maverick doctor. Depending on whom you talked to, that was either a bad thing or the sign of a revolutionary.

With a squad of siblings, Herb had cut his teeth playing a myriad of sports. A tenacious hunger for competition drove Herb from sport to sport. He even coerced his parents to allow a high-jump pit to be dug in the backyard of their Salt Lake home so he and his brothers could host neighborhood track meets. In spite of his all-around athletic prowess, Herb's great love was basketball. If he had to choose between basketball and eating, he would have gone hungry. And he would have been happy about it.

A cruel twist of fate nearly soured his love for the sport. He was only five feet two inches tall while attending junior high school. He was forced to try out for the school's basketball "C-squad," which had a height restriction so the boys on the team wouldn't have to compete with the more vertically endowed. The fact that one of his younger brothers towered over six feet led to obvious Mutt and Jeff comparisons. In an effort to fill his almost insatiable appetite for basketball, in addition to playing school ball, he turned to LDS Church basketball.

In Utah, LDS Church houses dotted the landscape, and in heavily populated areas one would have to travel no more than a mile in any direction to find a church building that featured a gym equipped with basketball standards. Leagues were formed and games were played with paid referees pitting one church congregation against another, often with their own team mascots. Competition was intense. At the time, the LDS Church leagues were rumored to be the largest basketball organization in the world. It was not unheard of to find some of the better players of the day opting out of high school basketball, and occasionally even college basketball, to compete in the church leagues. School and church teams frequently competed for prominence on the front page of many local sports sections.

For Herb, church basketball was an ideal place to exercise his devotion to the sport. The coaches defied contemporary and competitive wisdom in a show of fairness and played every player on the bench, regardless of size or skill. Herb overcame his diminutive stature through his voracious competitive nature, and in so doing found a way to hone his skills on the hardwood.

Serendipity rewarded his devotion. Between the tenth and eleventh grades Herb sprouted several inches, going from a third-stringer on his junior high team to the varsity starting five in high school. He kept growing, reaching a height of six feet four inches and eventually became the linchpin of his high school team.

As Herb continued to pursue his sport of choice during his freshman year at the University of Utah by continuing to actively participate in church leagues, Vadal Peterson noticed his name on the sports page of the *Salt Lake Tribune* and called him at home to personally extend an invitation to the Utes' tryouts.

That one phone call and a trip to Magna, Utah, to watch a high school basketball game represented Coach Peterson's entire recruiting effort for the 1943–44 team. Vadal wasn't known for his imagination, and that was as far as it took him. There was no one else to call, no up-and-coming stars that he knew of. He would just have to take whomever showed up in the girls' gym for the team. He hoped they at least would know how to dribble.

6

STITCHING
A TEAM TOGETHER

In the middle of every difficulty lies opportunity.

—ALBERT EINSTEIN

Tightening his worn laces, Wat noticed the crisscross pattern on the soles of his shoes. It had once looked like a fancy waffle, but it was now faded to smooth rubber, worn flat from the thousands of times his shoes had slid across the varnished hardwood. Even Wat couldn't count how many games they had seen, but he knew that if he wanted to play for the University of Utah's basketball team, they would have to be good enough. He had checked his bag twice on the way to the gym to make sure he had remembered them. The note on the board had stated emphatically that in order to play you needed your own shoes.

He had almost not even come to the basketball tryouts. Wat's love for the game hadn't faded, but he had been focused on his studies since the day he transferred to the university. If it weren't for the urging of a roommate, he wouldn't have even known about the tryouts. Wat had found living accommodations in an improvised dormitory that had been built adjacent to the football field. One of the half dozen young men with whom he shared his dorm room had seen the notice of the tryouts on the bulletin board and hadn't stopped mentioning it to him since.

Following his two years at Weber College, the nearby University of Utah was the only viable option for Wat to finish his engineering degree. Still living a modest life and unable to neglect his responsibilities to his mother and brothers, he would catch the Bamberger Railroad for the thirty-five mile ride home to Ogden every Friday, laundry in tow. Walking the less than half a block from the Union Pacific station to the barbershop, he would spend each weekend helping in the shop and generally acting as the family patriarch, standing in for his father. He would ride the Bamberger back to Salt Lake late on Sunday afternoons in time to finish his homework and be ready for classes on Monday morning.

On his way out of the locker room, with the sound of bouncing basketballs and squeaking shoes in the university gym beckoning, he stopped to look in a mirror. A wavy reflection of himself stared back, dressed in a worn pair of gym shorts and a used Weber College jersey. They were the only gym clothes he had, and it would probably be a long time before he got anything new.

As he rounded the corner into the gym, the clock on the wall read a few minutes before five o'clock and he trotted onto the court to make sure he was still technically early for the tryouts. There were already six or seven players gathered around the basket at the far end of the court shooting balls and warming up.

As he neared the group of players a few eyes turned to him. For a fraction of a second there was a hint of something behind the glances, but if there were anything to it, it faded quickly when someone passed him a ball and said, "Coach said we should warm up. He'll be back in a few minutes."

Wat stepped into the half circle of players facing the basket shooting set shots. He was the only one who wasn't white, not that anyone seemed to notice, and he couldn't help take note of how ridiculously tall everyone else was. To his right were two players that were almost a foot taller than him. Not only were they the same height, they also looked exactly alike. The one nearest to him paused between shots and stuck his hand toward Wat.

"I'm Fred, and that's my brother, Bob."

"Nice to meet'cha," Wat said. "My name's Wat."

"What?" the other brother called out. They seemed to have identical voices too.

"Wat. You can call me Wat."

The second twin trotted over and did a perfect imitation of his sibling's extended arm and quick handshake.

Over his shoulder, Wat heard the bang of a door and the sharp chirp of a coach's whistle. He turned around to see three serious-looking men walking toward them. One man walked a few steps ahead of the others with a whistle gripped in his well-spaced teeth. He wore gray sweatpants and a university sweatshirt that draped off his wide, plank-like shoulders. His eyes were sunk deep in his skull, his forehead swelled in a round, jutting brow that hung over his face like a cornice, and his face ended in a square jaw. If you were to judge his character by his looks, Vadal Peterson would have been judged a mean old curmudgeon.

"I'm Coach Peterson, and this is Pete Couch, my assistant coach," he said, motioning to the person on his left. "Keith Brown is gonna be our graduate manager," he continued, motioning to the other man. "Let's not waste any time."

Pulling a clipboard from under his arm, Vadal asked each player to state his name, where he was from, his major and his year in school. He nodded to the first player standing on his left and said, "Start us off, Sheff."

The player stood straight and replied, "Fred Sheffield, sophomore from Davis High, my major is premed—"

Vadal interrupted. "Boys, Fred was a starter from last year and is the current NCAA high-jump champion. Next."

Arnie was next in line. He puffed out his concave chest and stated, "Arnie Ferrin, freshman from Ogden High, two-time all-state, my major is business."

Herb Wilkinson was next to speak. He was a sophomore, but hadn't played basketball his freshman year. His major was premed, he was from Salt Lake City and he'd played ball at East High. Vadal thanked him for coming.

The next boy had a baby face and dark hair combed into a pompadour, and spoke just loud enough to be heard. "I'm Dick Smuin from

Cyprus High. I'm a freshman and my major is P.E. and coaching—"

Another loud bang sounded from the back of the gym, clipping off Dick's sentence. The door swung open and slammed hard against the hallway wall, startling Vadal. He looked up from his notes to see seven additional basketball hopefuls sprinting to join the team. "You're late," he shouted. "Sit on the bench and I'll deal with you later." In midsprint the seven players stopped, turned and sat dejectedly on the nearest bench.

Following the interruption it was Wat's turn. He stated his name and looked at Arnie, who nodded as if to acknowledge the fact that they were from the same town, even though this was the first time they had actually crossed paths. Wat stated that he was a junior and had played for two years at Weber College, and that his major was engineering.

Vadal didn't look up from his clipboard until after Wat was done. Then he raised his eyes to the last two players standing in the group and asked them to introduce themselves. They stepped forward at the same time, one of them speaking for both: "I'm Bob Lewis and this is my little brother Fred. We're freshmen with majors in engineering. We played at East High, a year after Herb."

Vadal stood staring at them for a long moment and finally said, "I'm bad with names and worse with faces. How can I tell you two apart?"

The twin on the right grinned and said, "It's easy coach. I'm the good-looking one."

Even from their first few moments of life, the Lewis twins were a surprise. On the night of their birth, their father, Robert S. Lewis, spent more than eight hours tracing a crooked route through the maternity ward. He had repeated the trek so many times that his swollen feet throbbed in his shoes. Each time he tried to sit down and relax, he found himself immediately back on his feet walking the same pattern on the well-worn linoleum floor. He eventually resorted to changing his route in minor ways to break up the monotony, walking in front of the couch instead of behind it.

Robert and his wife Lillian already had two daughters, two-year-old Mary and one-year-old Ruth. Both mom and dad were secretly hoping for a boy this time, and if they were lucky enough to get one, they both felt their family would be complete. Just as Robert was finishing another lap, a nurse motioned to him to follow her to the nursery. There, tucked snuggly in a blue blanket in a bassinet near the window, was Robert and Lillian's third child, a boy. They'd already decided that if the new addition were a boy they would name him Robert, after his father. The proud father bent toward the glass and cooed at his son.

He'd been there for forty-five minutes, gazing through the wire-reinforced window at the new arrival, when the nurse again entered. Wrapped up as he was in the sight of his new son, Robert didn't give much heed to the nurse as she walked toward the line of bassinets. It wasn't until she tapped on the window to gain his attention that Robert noticed that she was carrying another baby. In her arms, wrapped in another blue blanket, was a baby boy who looked like a carbon copy of Robert Junior.

Vadal walked in front of the line of young men, listening to their introductions and making notes on his clipboard. A few boys who had signed up hadn't shown, so the final tally—including the stragglers on the bench—was fourteen. He looked down at their feet and at least didn't see any penny loafers. "Well," he said through a crooked smirk, "it's a start. I guess you'll do."

Vadal believed firmly that conditioning and defensive excellence were the principals that were paramount in putting a competitive team on the floor, and that the creative instincts of the players would take care of the offense. Typically he played only five players, unless there were injuries. Those players had to be able to play the full forty minutes without a letdown in performance. Little time in practice would be wasted on offensive plays. Instead they would work on shooting fundamentals and defensive drills. He believed that every player should be able to shoot a set shot equally well from either side of the hoop, drive to the right and shoot with the right hand, drive to the left and shoot with the left hand, and drive the middle and shoot with either hand. It was a radical approach at the time, and it was hard to defend. Vadal's players needed to be comfortable with these skills from any position on the floor. The 1943–44 Utes would run what he called a "pickup man-to-man" defense, where there were no specific defensive assignments; rather, each of his players would pick up any man nearby that was similar in height each time the other team had the ball. It was not unlike a game of tag, where you went after the person who happened to be closest to you. Vadal's thinking was that if an opposing offensive player didn't know who would be defending him, it would be difficult to design an offensive scheme.

Putting the clipboard under his arm, Vadal explained the practice schedule. Workouts were to be held on Mondays and Wednesdays during the month of October; Mondays, Wednesdays and Fridays during November; and each weekday throughout the rest of the season. He warned the boys that it would be hard work, and he didn't want any of them turning into muscle-heads.

"The last thing you want is to spend so much time working your arms that you end up muscle-bound. You need to be in shape, but I don't want anyone on my team lifting weights or using medicine balls, so you can expect to run a lot at every practice. We'll do drill after drill until your feet are loose and your legs are strong."

All but two of the players were either premed or engineering students, and they had labs following class and were not available for practice until 5:00 p.m. The university had made a commitment to the military that the gym could be used for the Army Student Training Program starting at 6:00 p.m. each weekday evening, and so the team had only one hour of gym time per day. Every precious minute of their practices would have to be intense.

Vadal didn't say a word to the players for thirty minutes as he watched them scrimmage. He prowled along the sideline shaking his head and taking notes. Just before 6:00 p.m. he set the clipboard down and shouted, "That's it, hit the showers."

A few of the players had promise, but they were young. Four of his most promising prospects, Arnie Ferrin, Bob and Fred Lewis, and Dick Smuin, were freshmen and only eighteen years old. Herb Wilkinson was a sophomore scholastically, but a freshman as far as his athletic eligibility was concerned.

There were no surprises when it came to Fred Sheffield. He had been a track athlete his first year in college, and had been the starting center for the Utes' less-than-stellar 1942–43 basketball team. He was only six foot one but could leap out of his skin. That afternoon in practice he floated a head above everyone else while battling for rebounds. One year earlier he had won the NCAA high-jump championship with a jump of six feet eight inches. After practice, Vadal penciled him in for the second year in a row as the starting center.

It was at Fred Sheffield's fifth birthday party when it became obvious to his parents that he had unusual athletic gifts. His older race partner in the three-legged race couldn't keep up with his speedy legs; and in the foot race, running from the Sheffield's front yard around the neighbor's house and back, he beat his ten-year-old brother by three yards.

Fred didn't have to be coaxed into athletics; it was something that came to him naturally. When he was twelve years old he won the Junior Division of the Tri-State Pentathlon Games, and would go on to repeat that title for three more years. In 1939 he won the Senior Division, clearly outclassing his competition. But, as with Arnie and Wat, young Fred was not immune to tragedy.

Fred's father, also named Fred, was both the mayor and a successful business owner in Kaysville, Utah. His family was held in high esteem by citizens of the small farming town. Fred was in the seventh grade when his father suddenly passed away. Mr. Sheffield left his wife, Lyddia, and four children without a husband, father and any means of financial support. In order to meet their obligations, the family business was hastily sold to a buyer for far less than it was worth. Most of the proceeds of the sale were used to pay business debts, leaving very little to benefit the surviving Sheffields. To put food on the table, Lyddia worked at menial minimum wage jobs. She worked hard and provided the necessities but not the luxuries of life for her family.

Like Arnie and Wat, Fred insulated himself from the loss of his hero and mentor by becoming more focused on the things he did well, namely sports. At Davis High School he became an all-state basketball player. He was the state high-jump champion, the state long-jump champion and placed third in the high hurdles. He was the regional tennis champion, and went undefeated in matches during his high school career, but could not participate in the state tournament because it was held at the same time as the state track and field championships.

Fred entered the University of Utah in 1942 on a scholastic scholarship with a major in premed. In his first year at the university he found great success in both the classroom, where his grade point average was nearly 4.0, and on the athletic field, where he was a starter on the basketball team and earned all-American status as a track-and-field athlete.

He had noticed an announcement in the student newspaper that year promoting basketball tryouts. It was instantly obvious to Coach Peterson that even with Fred's relatively short stature he could use the six-foot-one leaper on his team, and he was immediately assigned the starting center position. The 1942–43 team was talent-poor and ended the season with a 10–12 record, but Fred enjoyed the competition and toyed with the idea of playing again his sophomore year. Since he would be the only returning player for the 1943–44 season, he assumed that another starting position was guaranteed.

The track and field coach at Utah had noticed Fred's leaping ability on the basketball court and encouraged him to join the track team in the spring of 1943. As a high jumper, Fred was undefeated in conference meets and traveled to Evanston, Illinois, to compete in the NCAA Track and Field Championships. He easily won the meet, outjumping his nearest competitor by three inches.

Fred had shown up the first day of basketball practice his sophomore year with few expectations for the team. Having first-hand experience with what had happened the preceding year, and knowing that the team wouldn't have the Field House to play in, he had a feeling the upcoming season wouldn't be one for the record books. As the "old man" on the team, he realized that this year's team could make last year's losing season look good by comparison. When he walked into the gym and saw nothing but unfamiliar faces, he was rightly worried.

As far as Vadal was concerned, the only sure thing about this year's team was Fred Sheffield. And there was one true surprise: Wat. He was a junior and had played well for two years at Weber College. Even though he was only five foot seven, he was tenacious and got into his opponent's face as if he were checking his five o'clock shadow. He was even shorter than Assistant Coach Couch, but was by far the quickest player Vadal had seen in years.

Vadal worried about Wat, though. Anti-Japanese sentiment was rampant at the time, and the Utes hoped to fill a number of open dates on their schedule with games against service teams. Players on those teams were soldiers first and basketball players second, and had been trained to hate the enemy. Since he played only five players most of the time, Vadal thought that by relegating Wat to a sixth-man role he could reduce or eliminate the problem altogether. He was a man with little prejudice, but he didn't know if he dared put a Japanese kid on the floor. There was no way to know how the boosters would respond, and the last thing Vadal wanted was more mail. The team this year would probably have more weaknesses than strengths, so he had to figure a way to keep Wat involved without giving him much game time.

Vadal walked out of the gym and down the hallway toward his office, muttering to Assistant Coach Couch. "We've got a bunch of young kids with no experience, except in high-jumping, and no team leader. But it doesn't really matter because we don't have any teams to play. I should'a been a math teacher."

Twice weekly during the month of October the team gathered for practice in the girls' gym, which featured a court half the size of a regulation basketball court. Under the direction of Coaches Peterson and Couch they practiced hard. There had been significant discussion among college basketball coaches and in sports sections of newspapers nationwide regarding the idea that freshmen didn't have the stamina or the strength to play a full forty-minute game under college rules. It wasn't until the early 1940s, with the drain of upperclassmen into military service, that freshmen were even *allowed* to play varsity basketball. Recognizing that freshmen would play major roles on his team, Vadal developed a conditioning philosophy that he felt would help get his youngsters into exceptional playing shape. When it came to exercise, Vadal didn't just work the kids out, he expounded the virtues of physical fitness, writing them down like jewels of wisdom:

> In the very early part of the season various calisthenics are given: abdominal exercises to churn the circulatory, respiratory and excretory systems; leg exercises to develop leg muscles and suppleness of the hips; shoulder exercises to relax

or loosen up shoulders and arms; wrist and finger exercises to develop complete relaxation of all muscles. The exercises most commonly used are: the side straddle hop; arms sidewards, upward swinging; arms circling; alternate toe touching; hopping in place or rope skipping; push ups, supporting the body on fingertips; sit-ups; and any other good exercise to develop the trunk and limbs. Of course, we use the usual games of keep away and twenty-one in daily workouts.

A large part of each practice was devoted to perfecting the one-handed set shot, which Vadal rightly thought was superior to the then-current practice of shooting two-handed from the chest. He felt that if his players shot one-handed from the field, they should also abandon the common free throw technique of the time: shooting underhanded with two hands from between the knees—what is now known as "granny" style. All of his players adapted well to the new free throw technique except Bob Lewis, who continued to shoot his free throws underhanded. Players were under strict orders to shoot for the rim rather than banking the shot off the backboard. Vadal had told them time and time again, "It's just more accurate on all shots from all angles, including the spot just behind and under the basket where you can't use the board. Also, shooting is more clear cut, less ragged and you won't get worried about English." Vadal didn't mention it, but he believed that shooting for the rim also caused less wear and tear on the backboards, and since the basketball budget was thin, he didn't want to have to replace them.

The players got into shape quickly. They learned their way around the university as well, as they ran through the hilly campus for hours every week. Vadal pushed them hard but didn't do anything that he felt might bulk up their physiques. He came into the gym before practice one day and found a few of the players tossing a medicine ball back and forth. His temper erupted and he yelled at them, telling them that they were ruining all the hard work they had done so far.

With his philosophy of placing a greater emphasis on defense, Vadal realized his greatest asset was Wat. Vadal even devised an entire drill around him. Taking turns, each player had to try to score against Wat. Vadal was thrilled to see how hard it was.

Just a few days before their first game, Vadal finally settled on the starting five: Arnie Ferrin, Bob Lewis, Fred Sheffield, Herb Wilkinson and Dick Smuin. Wat Misaka, Fred Lewis and four bench riders—Bill Kastellic, Jim Nance, T. Ray Kingston and another player of Japanese descent, Mas Tatsuno—would see little if any playing time. Vadal had battled with the idea but decided to play it safe and keep Wat on the bench—even though he was so focused in his play he had become his own practice drill. Each player who showed up for that first practice had earned a spot on the team, and there were just enough of them to fill the roster. Bill Pizza, Abe Bywater and Meeks Worthlin had been added to the roster initially, but were drafted into military service and had to report for active duty within weeks of tryouts. Vadal hadn't turned anyone away; he didn't have that luxury.

Vadal gave the university what it wanted: a basketball team. They had no home, no conference, and no one to play. Circumstances had forced him to start players who were young, gangly, and inexperienced. In normal circumstances most of them would have had permanent seats riding the pine. It wasn't much of a team, and the boys didn't look too promising on the court, but he was proud of what he'd cobbled together. Not unlike Dr. Frankenstein stitching together his creation out of the only things he was able to dig up, Vadal tried to put the spark of life in them.

He didn't know it at the time, but he too had created a monster.

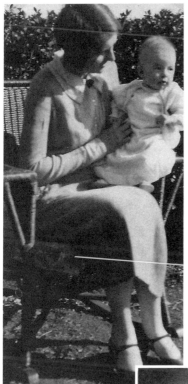

Ogden High School graduation photo of Arnie Ferrin. The next year he would be the first freshman to be named Most Outstanding Player in the history of the NCAA Basketball Tournament.

Ogden High School yearbook photo, courtesy Special Collections Department, Stewart Library, Weber State University.

Arnie Ferrin, four months old, with his mother Ellen. Ellen would pass away when Arnie was three, leaving him—her only child—to be raised by his grandparents C. P. and Ida Ferrin.

Courtesy Arnie Ferrin family.

Ogden High basketball team photo of Arnie Ferrin taken during his senior year.

Ogden High School yearbook photo, courtesy Special Collections Department, Stewart Library, Weber State University.

Ogden High School graduation photo of Wat Misaka. Wat would spend the next two years playing basketball at Weber College before transferring to the University of Utah.

Ogden High School yearbook photo, courtesy Special Collections Department, Stewart Library, Weber State University.

Weber College basketball team photo of Wat Misaka. At Weber College, Wat was a team leader in defense and scoring.

Courtesy Special Collections Department, Stewart Library, Weber State University.

A young Dick Smuin poses with a rooster on his family farm. Having him chase fighting cocks was one way Dick's father trained him to be a better ballplayer.

Courtesy Dick Smuin family.

Einar Nielson Field House was to be the Utes' home court during the 1943–44 season, but it was requisitioned by the army as a barrack to house troops.

Courtesy Special Collections Department, J. Willard Marriott Library, University of Utah.

Team photo of the 1943–44 "Blitz Kids." Back row, left to right: Coach Vadal Peterson, Fred Sheffield, Herb Wilkinson, Arnie Ferrin, Dick Smuin, Bob Lewis, Assistant Coach Pete Couch. Middle row: Jim Nance, Fred Lewis, Wat Misaka, Bill Kastellic, Manager Keith Brown. Front row, left to right: Mas Tatsuno, Ray Kingston. The university was only allowed to take nine players to the NIT. Bill Kastellic was drafted and reported for duty before the team left for the East Coast; Mas Tatsuno, the last man on the bench, did not make the trip.

Courtesy Arnie Ferrin.

Arnie Ferrin in his jersey number 22, which has been retired by the University of Utah.

Courtesy Arnie Ferrin.

Wat Misaka in his jersey number 21.

Courtesy *Deseret News* archives.

Wat Misaka, Arnie Ferrin, Herb Wilkinson, Dick Smuin and Bob Lewis pose for a publicity photo during the 1943–44 season.

Courtesy Special Collections Department, J. Willard Marriott Library, University of Utah.

*Fred Lewis goes
high for a rebound
in the girls' gym that
served as home court
for the Blitz Kids for
the first part of the
1943–44 season.*

Courtesy Special
Collections Department,
J. Willard Marriott Library,
University of Utah.

*Bob Lewis shooting
a free throw
during practice.*

Courtesy Special
Collections Department,
J. Willard Marriott Library,
University of Utah.

*Bob and Fred Lewis, two of the
"string bean kids," pose for a
publicity photo.*

Courtesy Special Collections Department,
J. Willard Marriott Library, University of Utah.

*Arnie Ferrin putting in
a layup during practice.*

Courtesy Special
Collections Department,
J. Willard Marriott Library,
University of Utah.

*Bill Kastellic working
on his defense.*

Courtesy Special
Collections Department,
J. Willard Marriott Library,
University of Utah.

*Arnie Ferrin (right, number 22) and Wat Misaka (left) battle
to control the ball during the University of Utah's National
Invitation Tournament loss to Kentucky in 1944.*

Courtesy *Deseret News* archives.

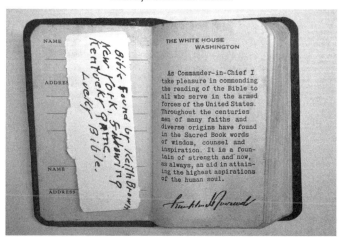

*The lucky bible found on the streets of New York by Keith Brown following
Utah's loss to Kentucky in the National Invitation Tournament.*

Photo by Josh Ferrin.

*Arnie Ferrin passes the ball to Wat Misaka (left) in the
1944 NCAA Championship game against Dartmouth. Bob
Gale of Dartmouth (number 4) watches the action.*

Courtesy Special Collections Department, J. Willard Marriott Library, University of Utah.

*Dartmouth's Bob Gale guards Arnie
Ferrin as the ball is tossed downcourt
during the NCAA finals in 1944.*

Courtesy Special Collections Department,
J. Willard Marriott Library, University of Utah.

*The Utes hoist Herb Wilkinson
moments after his game-winning
shot against Dartmouth.*

Courtesy Special Collections Department,
J. Willard Marriott Library, University of Utah.

Bob Lewis leaps for a rebound during the 1944 Red Cross benefit game that pitted Utah and St. John's University, the winners of the NCAA and NIT tournaments, against each other.
Courtesy Fred Lewis.

After returning from New York, the Utes traveled around Salt Lake City making public appearances and talking about their surprising victory. Several players who didn't travel to New York with the team joined them during their publicity tour.
Courtesy Special Collections Department, J. Willard Marriott Library, University of Utah.

The 1944 NCAA Championship trophy is now on display at the University of Utah's Jon M. Huntsman Center, where the current Utes play. The trophy features the names of all nine players who traveled to New York and the three coaches.

Photo by Sherry Ferrin.

The National Champion Runnin' Redskins pose with the NCAA trophy and their commemorative watches. Back row, left to right: Fred Sheffield, Wat Misaka, Fred Lewis, James Nance, Dick Smuin and Bob Lewis. Front row, left to right: Coach Vadal Peterson, Arnie Ferrin, Herb Wilkinson and Ray Kingston.

Courtesy Special Collections Department, J. Willard Marriott Library, University of Utah.

After weeks on the road, the Utes returned to Salt Lake City and were greeted with a ticker-tape parade. Here, Arnie Ferrin looks on at the crowds from the back of a convertible.

Courtesy Special Collections Department, J. Willard Marriott Library, University of Utah.

In 1947, three years after winning the NCAA Tournament, the University of Utah basketball team returned to New York to avenge their loss in the 1944 NIT. They beat Kentucky for the title. Wat Misaka (second from left), Arnie Ferrin (third from left), and other players lift Coach Vadal Peterson on their shoulders.

Courtesy Special Collections Department, J. Willard Marriott Library, University of Utah.

A bas-relief sculpture by Utah artist Ken Campbell commemorating the championships of 1944 and 1947 in the Einar Nielson Field House was accidentally destroyed during remodeling in the 1980s.

Courtesy Special Collections Department, J. Willard Marriott Library, University of Utah.

After his time with the Utes, Arnie played with the Minneapolis Lakers for three years, winning two championships. The 1950 championship team featured, from left to right: Slater Martin, Don Carlson, Herm Schaefer, Vern Mikkelsen, George Mikan, Jim Pollard, Arnie Ferrin and Tony Jaros.
Courtesy Arnie Ferrin family.

Sports continued to be a large part of Arnie's life after basketball, including golf. Here he receives a trophy at the Utah Open Amateur Golf Tournament in 1956.
Courtesy *Deseret News* archives.

Wat Misaka helped found a bowling league for Japanese Americans after they were denied the right to play in other leagues.
Courtesy *Deseret News* archives.

*Five former Utes players reunited in 1982 to commemorate their
surprising NCAA Championship. From left to right: Bob Lewis,
Dick Smuin, Arnie Ferrin, Ray Kingston and Wat Misaka.*

Courtesy *Deseret News* archives.

*Most of the 1943–44 team returned to their alma mater in 1989 when
the team was inducted into the University of Utah Hall of Fame. From
left to right: Dick Smuin, Arnie Ferrin, Wat Misaka, Fred Sheffield, Bill
Kastellic, Herb Wilkinson, Jim Nance, Fred Lewis and Bob Lewis.*

Courtesy *Deseret News* archives.

At a celebration of one hundred years of Utah basketball in 2008, Arnie Ferrin, Wat Misaka, Fred Sheffield, Herb Wilkinson and Fred Lewis stand in front of their 1944 championship trophy.

Photo by Sherry Ferrin.

Noting Arnie Ferrin's remarkable accomplishments at the dawn of the NCAA Tournament, the National Collegiate Basketball Hall of Fame inducted him in 2008 along with, from left to right, Charles Barkley, Jim Phelan, Billy Packer, Danny Manning, Dick Vitale and Nolan Richardson.

Photo by Sherry Ferrin.

SCRAPING TOGETHER A SCHEDULE

The key is not the will to win . . . everybody has that.
It is the will to prepare to win that is important.

— BOBBY KNIGHT

It was the fall of 1943. Keith Brown's shoulders drooped as he explained the situation to Coach Peterson. "There's just no one to play, I've tried just about—"

"Well, that's just not good enough, Keith," Vadal interrupted. "I chose you for this job. I don't care who shows up; go down to the retirement home and rally up some old ball hounds if you have to. Just get some teams to play."

Keith continued, "I've wired every school in the conference. None of them has a team this year and the conference won't let us play any service or independent teams." They sat in Vadal's office staring at one another. The coach didn't respond, forcing his fidgety assistant to find a way to break the awkward silence. Keith shifted in his chair and gave up the last detail, "We've got only one option, and it's not pretty."

"What is it?" Vadal asked.

"There are some informal teams on campus. The players are enlisted in the army but they're still students, so technically we can play them. But I'm not sure how it will play in the papers."

"Whaddya mean 'informal teams'? Coeds or something?" Vadal asked.

"Well," Keith continued, "they're part of the ASTP program."

"The guys who took over the Field House," Vadal noted.

Keith really didn't know much about the ASTP program, except that there were several companies on campus and their basketball teams were a step above those in the intramural program. There were three that were looking for games to play. At first Keith rejected the idea outright, but after appealing to the Skyline Conference for some leniency in their schedule and having his request rejected, he had no choice but to turn to anyone who would show up.

The Army Student Training Program was created in December 1942 to identify, train and educate academically talented college students. Utilizing major colleges and universities throughout the United States, the program provided a four-year education and military training. The purpose was to train officers who would fill leadership roles in the ongoing war effort and assist with the restoration of local governments in Nazi-occupied Europe.

The ASTP games were a desperate choice. Keith scheduled three games against three different squads. He had also told a team from the Eighteenth Replacement Wing, a military unit based nearby, that they could get together for a scrimmage, but after his conversation with Vadal he decided to call it a "game"; it was easier to play the team and try to get permission later. He knew the conference wouldn't approve, but he had no choice. His hope was to convince the conference to allow them to bend the rules that kept college teams from playing the more experienced service squads and independent teams.

The Utes had shown real dedication by fielding a team when no other team in the conference had, and Keith could only hope that would play well in their favor. He sent another series of wires to conference headquarters, emphasizing the dedication of the players and the value the game of basketball had to them in a time of war. He hoped that the conference would respond quickly or they were going to have a short season.

Keith had spent a lot of time trying to build a schedule from scratch, but he hadn't found a place for the Utes to play their home games, and so they continued to use the girls' gym. Before their first game, Vadal invited the varsity squad from nearby East High School to scrimmage against the Utes. To his horror the final score was shockingly close— the Utes won, but just barely. The team failed to connect on most of their shots and played as if they had never practiced together. Vadal was so livid that he left the gym after the game without a word to his players or staff.

There were few expectations for the team in their first game of the season against the group of ballers in the Eighteenth Replacement Wing on campus. No reporters showed up, and there weren't any officials from the university. The few fans that attended, mostly friends and family of the players, lined the sides of the court, standing just a few inches behind the sidelines. Vadal, Keith and Coach Couch were anticipating disaster. They had no reason to expect anything else from a team that had almost lost to an average high school squad. This could be the kind of game to slip silently into history, happily forgotten in favor of better years. But it was also a situation ripe with potential.

The players hadn't thought too much about it; they were happy just to be playing ball. Something came over the starting five as they trotted onto the court. Maybe it was the crowd, small but supportive; maybe it was the pressure the team was feeling. Whatever it was, it brought them together in a way Vadal could only describe as magical. The Utes' defense was arresting, and the offense jelled and scored at will. After the game Vadal walked over to Pete and asked if he could explain what had happened; they had played like a completely different team from the mess he had seen in the scrimmage against the high schoolers.

The next three games were against the ASTP teams, and by some miracle the Utes trounced each one. They had heard from too many experts that they were just too young and inexperienced to be anything but cannon fodder even for average local recreation teams. Even with Arnie on the bench for the first two games with a shoulder injury, none of the first four games were in doubt. The defense was tenacious and kept the opposition off-balance, not knowing who was defending whom. The freewheeling offense, without any set plays, had the opposing defenders constantly confused. The Utes were 4–0 after their first four games, and had won the games by a cumulative score of 246–76.

As Wat and Arnie walked out of the girls' gym following their latest victory, Wat said, "I didn't think we would win more than four games all season, let alone our first four." Arnie shook his head and said softly in reply, "I didn't think we'd win any."

Vadal, not being one to hand out unearned compliments, seemed generally pleased with the team's effort—especially Fred Sheffield's. With his uncanny leaping ability, Sheff had cleaned the backboards of rebounds and led the team in scoring.

With Keith able to schedule only two games in December, practice for the next month would be intense and focused. The coach still had some concerns he wanted to iron out before the team started the remainder of their schedule, when they would be playing more experienced service and AAU teams. Bob Lewis, the tallest player on the team (edging out his twin brother by less than an inch), defended well, but Vadal was concerned about his quickness and devised a plan to speed up his slow feet. During practice he assigned Bob to defend Wat, the team's smallest and by far quickest player. The goal was for Bob to stay within three steps of Wat at all times.

Vadal barked at Bob from the sidelines each time Wat got an advantage in position on the floor. Each time Vadal yelled, Bob tried harder, but ultimately Wat's natural quickness was too much for him to handle. One time Wat drove around Bob to the basket and attempted an easy layup. Bob collected the ball as it bounced off the rim and tried to dribble before making an outlet pass. The ball bounced off his foot and ricocheted under the bleachers. Vadal's eyes dropped; he wasn't able to watch another second of Bob's stumbling clown routine. When the players came back down the floor he blew his whistle. He walked up to Fred Lewis, the closest Lewis brother he could find, grabbed him by his sweaty practice jersey and stood six inches from his nose while berating the lanky ballplayer and then sending him to the shower. Fred tried to argue with the coach that he had the wrong brother, but Vadal wasn't listening. Fred realized the futility of arguing any further, so he shut up, grabbed his bag and walked by his smiling brother Bob on the way to the shower.

Robert Lewis, Bob and Fred's father, had been hired by the University of Utah in 1912 to develop its School of Mines and Engineering. The Lewis family lived on the east bench of Salt Lake City near the university campus. Just behind their home was Victory Park, a large expanse of trees and grass that included a number of tennis courts. Robert, a former college athlete, held the belief that physical activity should be part of the proper upbringing of his children.

In spite of being tall and thin as youngsters, both twins showed an early aptitude for sport. At the age of ten, Bob and Fred, along with their older sister Ruth, started playing tennis as a summer pastime. Both twins had a strong competitive desire, and through hard work quickly learned that they could beat most of the children who dared to compete with them.

Hay fever was the curse of the Lewis family during the summer months. Since Robert didn't teach during those months, the family traveled to Arcadia, California, where they rented a home from Robert's brother for the summer. In Southern California, where the offending allergens were absent, the Lewis children could participate in athletic pursuits and not be hindered by constantly runny noses.

Freedom from school provided the twins the opportunity to do what they enjoyed most. Days would start early as herds of children would gather and bike to the local elementary school. There they would play tennis until it got too dark, at which point they would ride home. At the end of one particularly long and warm day on the tennis court, after Fred had played 118 games, he tried to jump the net to shake hands with a defeated foe—but didn't quite make it. His skinny legs were so tired they were unable to clear the top of the net. He caught his toes in the net and fell awkwardly onto the opposite side of the court. In addition to a terribly bruised ego, he suffered a dislocated shoulder and a broken arm.

As Bob and Fred entered their teen years, golf was added to the complement of summer sports at which they excelled. They now carried tennis racquets, golf clubs and swimming suits with them as they rode their bikes to nearby Santa Anita Park. They would play nine holes of golf in the morning, swim for several hours before playing two or three sets of tennis, finish the day by playing another nine holes of golf and then ride three miles home.

Each fall the Lewis family would return to Salt Lake City. Bob and Fred attended the Stewart Training School on the campus of the University of Utah, where they enjoyed typical identical-twin antics at the expense of friends and teachers. In geography class one fall day they sat in each other's seats to fool the teacher. Because the two were just as competitive scholastically as they were athletically, Fred decided to get the upper hand on his brother. Each time the teacher asked a student to answer a question, Fred, posing as his brother Bob, would raise his hand to volunteer—then deliberately give the wrong answer.

The twins found that they not only looked identical, but they frequently shared the same thoughts. In the ninth grade they were in the same English class, though they sat on opposite sides of the classroom. After turning in an assignment one day, each twin was called to the front of the room and accused of copying each other's work. The teacher presented the two papers as evidence: the twins had written nearly identical papers, without having discussed the topic between themselves beforehand.

The Stewart School had an excellent athletic program and competed against other junior high schools in the area. Bob and Fred had spent time playing driveway basketball against each other and had played a lot of playground ball. The idea of playing competitive basketball for Stewart against other schools was a thought that was appealing to both brothers. In preparation for the upcoming season, each morning they got up early enough to go to school and shoot a hundred foul shots each before class.

Both twins were named starters at Stewart and together led the team to several successful seasons. In the eighth grade, while playing crosstown rival Judge Memorial, Fred was assigned to defend the league's leading scorer, a young man who had an ego that matched his ability to score. Fred stuck to the Judge Memorial star like a burr to a fuzzy sock. At halftime, Fred had held him scoreless and rendered him ineffective as a playmaker. As the teams were taking their positions on the floor to begin the third quarter, the frustrated young man walked up to Bob and, believing he was Fred, slugged him in the belly, doubling him over and leaving him gasping for air.

Both of the brothers had a keen mind and an aptitude for math. They worked hard in school, and at high school graduation each boasted a 4.0 grade point average. They both had plans on attending the University of Utah and pursuing degrees in engineering. The decision pleased their mother and father, since they could live at home and avoid the extra expense of room and board. They assumed that, although they were each nearly six feet four inches tall and had been successful in high school athletics, only recreational basketball would fit into their busy college schedules. They looked forward to playing golf, doing some skiing in the winter and playing competitive tennis during the summer months.

During the early fall of 1943, during the twins' first year at the university, a classmate mentioned to Bob that he had seen a notice posted in the girls' gym announcing varsity basketball tryouts. After school the brothers walked to the gym and signed their names to the short list of potential players, thinking at least it might be fun to try out.

The next two games for the Utes were road games and Vadal was anxious to see how his youthful brood would play away from the confines of their familiar gym. On December 4, the Utes traveled to Wat and Arnie's hometown of Ogden to play Weber College, where Wat had been a star the year before. Utah won easily, 63–25, but Wat played more minutes than Vadal felt comfortable with. Next they traveled to Camp Kearns to take on the Second Air Force team, which provided a better test. With Sheff scoring sixteen points and Herb seven, combined with Utah's hawkish defense led by Herb and Bob, Utah beat the air force team by ten.

Following practice one evening in early January, Keith knocked on Vadal's office door with bad news. There were just two more games scheduled for the remainder of the season: one on January 4 against Fort Douglas and one on January 6 against the Wendover Bomber Squadron. After that, unless there were divine intervention, the season would be over. Keith had sent out multiple letters of inquiry to AAU, college and service teams in Utah, Colorado and Wyoming, but to date nothing had been confirmed and prospects were less than promising.

During the early games of the season fan support had been minimal, typically with fewer than fifty spectators scattered along the sidelines at home games. As the team began piling up victories, fan interest began to skyrocket. Soon the girls' gym was packed with spectators eager to see the Utes play. The local newspapers, which hadn't even covered any of the early games, were starting to give proper press to the team's success.

After the initial struggles in patching the team together and the team's early success on the court, it would be a shame if the season faded away for the simple reason they couldn't find teams to play. Keith told Vadal he would contact all potential opponents once again. The hardest thing for Vadal wasn't the fact that he thought this team could be great; he was more realistic than that. It was that these kids just seemed to love playing ball, win or lose. They were gym rats. He loved their attitude and wanted to be part of it.

The team from Fort Douglas was stocked with veteran ballplayers. Dale Rex had been the starting center at Brigham Young University for two years before enlisting in the military. He was six feet seven inches tall and had dominated the post position during his college years. They also had three all-state high school players from Idaho, a former all-star player from Mesa Junior College in Colorado, Swede Glover, and former Montana State player Dan Mizner. This game would be the toughest test yet for the young and inexperienced but determined Utes.

The girls' gym was packed with cheering students who had come to see their team play its last game on campus. To accommodate the growing crowds and to avoid scheduling conflicts with the military, any further games that Keith managed to schedule for the team would be played off-campus at the Deseret Gym in downtown Salt Lake City.

The veteran players from Fort Douglas initially proved to be too much for the youngsters from Utah, who trailed the service team at the end of the first quarter. By halftime, however, the Utes smothering defense had contained the offensive attack of Rex and his teammates, and the Utes were up by a point. The hours spent on conditioning proved to be the difference in the second half for the seemingly tireless Utes. Scoring was spread evenly between Ferrin, Sheffield, Smuin and Wilkinson. Wat played a role in shutting down Fort Douglas's offense with his tenacious defensive effort. At the final buzzer the score was 41–25 in favor of the young Utes.

Meanwhile Keith's scheduling woes had abated. In fact, it was as if someone had opened the headgates of an irrigation canal and turned on the water, as game opportunities suddenly came streaming in. Keith was so excited the season would continue that he scheduled *two* games for January 15 against two different opponents: Weber Navy, a military team from Weber College, was scheduled to meet the Utes at 6:00 p.m., and Idaho Southern would play them at 8:15. A double-header in baseball was commonplace, but in basketball it was suicide. But at this point in the season, when there had been a dearth of teams to play, there was no way Keith was going to turn down a game.

Vadal's face blanched, then turned scarlet, when Keith told him of the upcoming doubleheader. He was a man who freely and frequently verbalized his displeasure when things didn't go well with regard to his team, and this year that had been the case more often than not. Although he liked Keith and thought he did an outstanding job as team manager, scheduling two games in one night was insane and Keith alone was to blame for this imprudence.

Weber Navy had a decent ball club, but Vadal felt confident his team could beat them on most nights. Idaho Southern was one of a number of college teams in the country that had actually been able to improve their team as a result of the war. They had lost a number of good players to the draft and enlistment, but the team had been the fortunate recipient of six outstanding ballplayers who enrolled in the school through the Navy V-12 program. The team was loaded with upperclassmen, many of whom had starred on their previous college teams. This year Idaho Southern had the best team they had put on the floor in fifteen years. Even with fresh legs the young Utes would be underdogs.

On January 14, just one day before the doubleheader, Vadal loudly explained to Keith that he would have to find another team to play in the first game against Weber Navy. Keith had already announced the doubleheader and the newspapers would be publishing the story the next morning. He quickly walked to the ASTP administration building on campus, desperate with the hope that one of the ASTP companies would be willing to play the first game of the evening. Lady Luck smiled on Keith: Company D jumped at the opportunity to fill in for the overbooked Utes.

The Deseret Gym, the Utes' new home, was built in 1910 and included a swimming pool, tennis courts, handball courts, a full-size basketball court and a running track. The basketball court was surrounded by bleachers, which when full held between 2,500 and 3,000 tightly packed fans. The bleachers extended out to within twelve inches of the sidelines. A three-lane running track was suspended approximately twenty feet above the court. The curves of the track encroached into the airspace above the four corners of the basketball court, while the straight portions of the track were tucked in nicely above the bleachers. The Utes would have to get used to the eccentricities of the gym's layout and share court time with all of the community leagues, but at least they had a place to play.

At 7:45 p.m. on January 15 the team walked onto the floor of Deseret Gym to warm up. It was just thirty minutes before their game with the Idaho Southern Bengals and the first chance they'd had to even practice at the gym. Testing the bounce of the floor, Arnie took the ball and dribbled to one of the corners, spun and faced the basket, and shot. "Thunk." The ball hit the bottom of the running track and bounced back to the floor halfway through its flight to the basket. He laughed and shook his head in amazement, then tried the shot two more times from the same spot with similar results. It was impossible to hit a shot from that position on the floor. He scooped up two more balls as he trotted over to the other starters, tossed them the balls and challenged them to shoot the ball from the same position and make a basket. Each shot produced the same "thunk" and ended with the ball rolling on the floor halfway to the basket. Standing with his teammates looking up at the bottom of the track, Sheff had an idea. They huddled together and decided to take advantage of their defensive "sixth man"—the architect who'd designed the building.

Sheff easily controlled the opening tip of the game. He batted the ball to Arnie, who dribbled to the right of the foul line and started the scoring with a set shot from fifteen feet. Idaho Southern's go-to shooter, Jay Jensen, brought the ball into the frontcourt for the Bengals where he was picked up by Herb, who forced him deep into the corner. Once Jensen had picked up his dribble, Herb backed off the pressure just a little. The Idaho guard, sensing a softening of Herb's defense, lofted a shot from just inside the sideline. His jaw dropped in amazement as he watched the ball ricochet off the underside of the running track. Utah's bench erupted in cheers as the players jumped up and down. Jensen raised his arms in protest, but the referee waved away his argument and signaled him to play on.

The Utes continued to pressure the Bengals' offense by switching defensive assignments each time down the court. At halftime Utah led the veteran team from Idaho 27–13. During the second half Utah continued to dominate play, with Arnie scoring consistently. The game ended 54–43 in favor of the Utes, who played only their starting five for the entire game. Arnie led all scorers with seventeen points.

Utah's once barren schedule quickly filled up. It seemed everyone wanted to take on the undefeated Utes. Keith scheduled a tough Ecker Studio team for a home game on January 22, and the first extended road trip of the year to Colorado and Wyoming. The Utes would play at Colorado College on January 28, Fort Logan in Denver on January 29 and Fort Warren in Cheyenne on January 31. To help defray the costs of travel for the team, Colorado College guaranteed the Utes $250 for the game, and Fort Logan and Fort Warren guaranteed them $50 and $75, respectively. Tentative dates for an additional six games were penciled in and would be confirmed when the Utes returned home.

Finally it appeared the Runnin' Redskins would have a full season of games to play.

PERSEVERANCE PAYS OFF

My strength lies solely in my tenacity.

—LOUIS PASTEUR

Ecker Studio was an AAU powerhouse and perennial champion of the Intermountain League. The team was sponsored by the owner of a local photography studio whose interest in basketball had turned into fanaticism. It was composed of handpicked former college players from the area who still had a competitive fire and found the Ecker Studio team provided a way for them to relive their former days of glory. Each player had to be a well-rounded contributor to the team on both offense and defense. They were big, strong and quick. They could shoot well and played tough. Their plan for their game against Utah was to outmuscle the skinny kids and optimize the physical advantage they had. They planned on badly beating the Utes—by one definition of the word or the other.

For the second game in a row, the pungent Deseret Gym was tightly packed with fans. Tickets for the game were sold out and fans arriving late to the game were turned away. Those who couldn't find a seat stood along the suspended track above the court, or sat with their legs dangling from the track over the bleachers. When the

11–0 Utes took the floor, a loud roar from the excited patrons filled the tiny gym.

Vadal's exercise regime had paid off and the conditioned college players were easily able to outhustle the older and bigger Studio team. As an equalizer, the Studio team grabbed their opponents and threw elbows whenever they thought they could gain an advantage. Dick immediately knew the game would be more of a brawl than one of finesse. Fighting for an early rebound against a Studio player, he was greeted by a strategically placed elbow to the side of his head. He came crashing to the floor, landing hard on his chest. The Utes understood that even if they won the game the black-and-blue memories would linger.

By halftime the skill and quickness of the Utes had garnered them a 26–18 lead. But the physical nature of the game wore them down in the second half. In spite of the pounding his kids received, Vadal continued to play the fewest players possible, using only six bone-tired and bruised players. Arnie played a brilliant game. Although manhandled throughout, he led all scorers with twenty-one points, and the Utes won by their narrowest margin of the season, 46–44.

Following practice one cold evening late in January, Dick climbed off the train and walked the two blocks to his home, his coat collar turned up to protect his neck and face from the windblown ice crystals. He entered the house to find his father, Lavell, and mother, Ted, gone for the evening. He hung up his coat and walked into the living room, where the mail sat resting on a small end table. He placed his feet on the warm heater vent and thumbed through the stack of five letters. The third letter in the stack, addressed to him, carried a return address for the Selective Service System. It was the same letter that was being sent to thousands of young American men each week. Dick opened the letter and saw a simple salutation that said "Greetings," followed by an order to report in two weeks for induction into the military. He had always intended to serve his country, and hoped to one day wear a navy seaman's uniform. However, the thought of having to leave school now, while the team was undefeated, made him nauseated. As it turned out, teammate Bill Kastellic opened a similar letter the same day.

Draft notice in hand, Dick entered Vadal's office, tossed the letter on the coach's cluttered desk and told him the news. Vadal calmed the upset young man and told him he felt certain that by appealing to the local draft board he could defer his entry into the military until after winter quarter was over in mid-March. This would give him the opportunity to complete his school work and see the end of regular season play for the Utes. Dick and his father wrote the letter of appeal and the draft board found in favor of Dick and the Utes, postponing the date Dick was to report until the first part of April. Bill Kastellic's basketball season, however, was over. He reported for military duty and the Utes lost an important second-team player.

The young kids from Utah were coming together as a team; their undefeated record was proof of that. However, because all but three of the players lived at home—Arnie, Wat and Sheff were the only ones who lived on campus—they didn't spend much time together off the court. Their education was the paramount reason each of them attended the university. Evenings after practice were spent in academic pursuits rather than enjoying social activities. The trip to Colorado and Wyoming was the first opportunity for the team members to become acquainted off the court.

A natural friendship had developed between Arnie and Wat, the two Ogden boys, and Vadal hoped that by assigning them to share the same hotel rooms, racial tension would be avoided. His concerns were unfounded, though. Every player looked at Wat as nothing more or less than just another team member. He was their friend and teammate, and there was an unspoken agreement that they would all be ready to defend him.

Just prior to boarding the train for Colorado, the team held a brief meeting in the lobby of the Denver & Rio Grande railroad station. Vadal had his players unpack their bags and show him that they had each remembered to bring their basketball shoes. He sternly reminded them not to lose them; if they did they wouldn't play.

Vadal was a principled man and felt his players should hold themselves to the same moral standards he did. Smoking was prohibited, as was drinking alcohol and playing cards for money. He understood that the boys needed to entertain themselves on an overnight train trip, and playing cards was acceptable as long as no money changed hands. Being cerebral kids, most of the players preferred playing bridge to poker, and were good at the game. Wat had been tutored in cards during his days at Weber College by his good friend Roy Yoshioka. His aptitude at bridge was equaled on the team only by Arnie, who had gained considerable experience playing cards in his spare time at the Beta House on campus. Although the Lewis brothers were excellent basketball and tennis players, their mastery of bridge was limited to their imaginations; in reality their card-playing skills were below average.

Bob and Fred had challenged Arnie and Wat to a game early in the evening. Following their meal in the dining car, they sat and played for several hours, with Arnie and Wat winning most games easily. Finally Vadal asked them to go to bed, reminding them they had a ball game to play the next night. The Lewis brothers, being competitive by nature, didn't want to end the evening on a losing note and coaxed Arnie and Wat into continuing. After the rest of the players and coaching staff had gone to bed, Arnie and Wat quietly entered Bob and Fred's Pullman car. The four players climbed into one berth and closed the curtain behind them. Bob and Fred sat against the wall of the car, while Arnie and Wat sat with their backs to the curtain facing the twins.

By 12:30 in the morning, the twins had played well enough to win two games. Arnie leaned back to stretch his legs and looked up into a mirror placed in the corner of the ceiling. Surprised, he squinted, rubbed his eyes and looked up at the mirror again. He could clearly see Fred's cards. He gently kicked Wat's leg and motioned with his head to the mirror on Wat's side of the berth. As Wat gazed into the mirror, Bob's cards clearly came into view. Wat gave Arnie a knowing wink, and the luck of the Lewis brothers suddenly changed. At 4:00 a.m., with a tone of utter disgust in his voice, Bob threw his cards onto the mattress and shouted, "I quit! I can't believe we haven't won a game in three and a half hours." Struggling to keep from laughing out loud, Arnie and Wat promised a rematch and quietly slid into their berth to get a few hours sleep before they arrived in Colorado Springs.

Vadal had scheduled an early afternoon practice at the Colorado College Field House. He wanted the team to take some shots on the unfamiliar court and have a light defensive strategy session. Nothing hard; he just wanted the team to break a sweat. With Bill Kastellic now in the military and the Utes' traveling squad reduced to an odd-numbered nine, Vadal was presented with a problem he had never faced before: there weren't enough players to run a practice. There wasn't an easy solution to the problem. Vadal was too old to practice with the team, and Keith, although he traveled with the team, wasn't an athlete. The only option Vadal had was to ask Coach Couch to dress and practice with the squad. Pete Couch could be described as a mobile retaining wall. He approached six feet two inches in height and was quite wide. The assistant coach worked hard in his spare time to stay in playing shape.

In practice, Bob kept trying to keep pace with the speedy Wat. Over the course of the season his foot speed had improved. Vadal figured that the talented but skinny Arnie needed a little more muscle to battle the older and physically more mature players the Utes would be facing, so in practice he was assigned to guard Pete. Vadal specifically ordered Pete to lean on, hold and push Arnie anytime the opportunity presented itself. He wanted Arnie to earn every inch of floor he crossed and to work hard for every rebound he pulled down. By the end of practice Vadal could sense that Arnie, Wat and the Lewis twins were dragging, so he sent the team back to the hotel to rest before the game.

The Colorado College Tigers basketball roster was filled completely by navy and marine active-duty servicemen, including veteran players from several universities in the western United States. They were undefeated against college opponents. Because of their age and experience, many believed that the Tigers would hand the Utes their first loss of the season. The local newspaper had quoted Vadal as saying that "he didn't expect his inexperienced freshman club to win a single game on the road trip." He followed that up by admitting, "Oh well, it won't hurt them to get beat. That is part of the lesson athletics teaches."

The game tipped off on Friday at 7:30 p.m. in the packed Field House on the campus in Colorado Springs. As usual Sheff controlled the tip, which Herb quickly gathered in. He dribbled into the frontcourt and threw a bounce pass to Bob, who cut through the key and made an uncontested layup to start the scoring. Arnie scored the next six points for Utah to extend the lead further. Playing aggressive defense, Bob picked up two quick fouls, which angered Vadal because he'd once again planned on playing only his starting five. Wat quickly substituted in for Bob, prompting a number of calls from the crowd that filtered down to the court from the bleachers. Wat seemed entirely unaware of his detractors—or perhaps he just ignored them. Arnie, however, used the insults as motivation to continue his scoring rampage. Just before halftime Vadal brought Bob back in for Wat, and he immediately picked up a reach-in foul defending a quicker player. The first half ended with the Utes leading 23–14.

In the locker room at halftime, Vadal was incensed with Bob's three first-half fouls. Not being able to tell the twins apart he grabbed Fred, the nearest Lewis twin, and scolded him in front of the entire team, accusing him of being lazy on defense. Though he hadn't played a single minute of the game, Fred didn't seem at all surprised by Vadal's mistake. He had been wrongly accused for his brother's miscues before, and understood it was no use to argue with the raging coach.

Once Vadal had finished his tirade, Pete, unable to control his laughter, took Vadal by the arm and said, "Coach, this is Fred; Bob is over there."

The embarrassed Vadal turned to Bob, pointed his finger and yelled, "And the same goes for you!"

Arnie continued to dominate the scoring in the second half, while Utah's defense bewildered the team from Colorado, holding their top scorers far below their season averages. Sheff controlled the boards easily on both ends of the court. The game ended with the score in favor of the underdog Utes, 48–34. Arnie led all scorers again with a game-high twenty-three points, followed by Herb with eleven.

The team spent that night at the Antlers Hotel, just a few blocks from campus and a short bus ride to the train station. They left early the next morning to travel to Denver to play Fort Logan on Saturday evening, January 29.

The game with Fort Logan would be played on the military base in the newly constructed post gym. The team was definitely not the pride and joy of the base commander, and in fact had been the target of many less-than-complimentary comments by the military leadership of other bases throughout the Rockies. The Fort Logan team boasted only one player with any previous major college experience:

Hugh Salisbury, who had played freshman ball at Purdue University before being drafted into the army. The team had struggled badly against their opponents and had a losing record. While two games on back-to-back nights was better than two games in one night—as Keith had scheduled earlier in the year—on Monday night the Utes would play the best team they had played all year. Realizing that his starters needed some rest before the Monday night game at Fort Warren, Vadal told his team before the game that, in a break from his usual approach, everyone on the team would play.

He started his regular five for the game, but substituted freely once it became apparent that the Fort Logan team had an undistinguished reputation for good reason. Sheff easily controlled the boards, and for the game led all scorers with twenty points. Arnie scored twelve while playing little more than half the game. Wat, coming off the bench, forced several Fort Logan turnovers and received a token applause at the end of the game from the sparse crowd, who had initially appeared hostile toward the Ute guard. Utah won going away, 55–38.

The Utes spent Saturday night and Sunday at Fort Logan. The base had agreed to provide room and board for the team for two nights in addition to the $50 guarantee for playing the game. Arnie and Wat shared a bunk bed in the barrack that housed the team, which was isolated from the rest of the military population. Some of the servicemen were overt about their discontent over the idea of a person of Japanese descent staying at the military base. Walking through the base Wat caught more than a few hard stares and heard a fair amount of epithets. On Sunday the entire team stuck close to him and spent the whole day together. If there were trouble, Arnie wondered how eight skinny kids from Utah were going to defend their teammate from the entire military force of Fort Logan. As usual, Wat seemed unaffected by the tension felt by his teammates.

Despite a fair amount of intimidation—but luckily no incidents—the team left the stressful surroundings of Fort Logan and traveled to Cheyenne, Wyoming, on Monday morning. They arrived at the Union Pacific station and rode a bus to Fort Warren, where once again they would be unpopular guests at a military base.

The Utes were substantial underdogs in their upcoming game against the team from Fort Warren. The basketball gods must have been working overtime to assemble the talented group of basketball players who came together on the small military base on the cold plains of Wyoming just outside Cheyenne. Whereas the team from Fort Logan was the laughingstock of the Service League, the team from Fort Warren had won the Service League Championship the year before, and would do the same in 1944. Like the Utes, Fort Warren was undefeated, and had not won a game by less than fifteen points.

Their roster was loaded with former college stars and professional players from across the country, most notably Ermer Robinson and Jules Rivlin. Robinson was a six-foot-two-inch guard/forward who had gained regional recognition as a spectacular high school player in San Diego, California. He was a great scorer and an outstanding leaper. His basketball prowess was aided by the fact that he was a superb natural athlete. One weekend in the early 1940s, the Harlem Globetrotters were playing in San Diego. Abe Saperstein, the owner of the team, walked into a game at San Diego High School intending to do some scouting for potential players. He was immediately impressed with Robinson and offered him a job on the spot playing for the Trotters. Ermer played for the Globetrotters from 1942 until he was drafted into the military and stationed at Fort Warren. Following the war, he would eventually return to the Globetrotters, for whom he would star for fourteen seasons.

The five-foot-eleven-inch Rivlin was a player/coach for the powerful Fort Warren team. On the court he was the perfect complement to Robinson. While Ermer was a scoring machine with a silky shot who could slash across the key for a rebound or a put back, Jules was a heady ballplayer who also had the ability to score at will. He had honed his finely tuned skills as a three-year starter at Marshall College in West Virginia. As a sophomore he'd set a single-season Marshall scoring record. In his junior year he was the second leading scorer in all of college basketball, and led the Thundering Herd to a 25–4 record. In his senior year he became Marshall's first basketball all-American and finished his college career with 1,093 points. Before entering the military he played professional ball with the Akron Goodyear Wingfoots, and in 1943 was named an AAU all-American. After serving his country, Jules would return to the professional ranks, retiring in 1948.

Arriving at Fort Warren, the Utes' bus traveled to a small wooden barrack that stood apart from the rest of the military housing. The bunk-lined room had sleeping quarters for about twenty-five men, so the nine players, two coaches and Keith spread out and made themselves comfortable. The team gathered for dinner at 5:00 p.m., two and a half hours before game time. Just as they did the day before in Colorado, the team surrounded Wat and walked into the mess hall. Soldiers' heads turned to watch Wat enter the mess line closely accompanied by a group of tall, thin young men. From the back of the room someone yelled, "Sorry, no rice today!" Harsh voices sounded from around the hall, but Wat again showed tolerance for those who were intolerant and seemed unaffected by their ill-mannered hosts. Arnie and the rest of the team made mental notes of the comments and decided that the basketball court was the place to take revenge.

The base gymnasium was packed with 2,500 members of the military and 150 or so citizens of Cheyenne. They had braved the steel-cold night to watch the two unbeaten teams battle in what would be a classic game. The Utes were the only all-civilian college team remaining west of the Rocky Mountains. The local sportswriters didn't give the team from Salt Lake a chance against the veteran Quartermasters.

Being unusually verbose, Vadal said to his team before they took the court, "You boys are undefeated, and in order to keep it going you will have to play your best game of the season. Now let's go." Not a pep talk for the ages, but for Vadal it was pretty good.

During warm-ups, jeers erupted from the crowd each time Wat touched the ball. He seemed to have the ability to put the distraction out of his mind and focus on the task at hand. Arnie and Sheff, however, found the disrespect for their teammate disgusting and used the verbal abuse as motivation. Arnie hoped that during the game Wat would have the opportunity to play, and play well.

With Sheff jumping center, the remaining four starters crouched around the center circle. Sheff jumped a good five inches higher than Fort Warren's center and easily controlled the tip, which was immediately snatched from Herb's hands by Jules Rivlin. Rivlin fired an overhead pass to Robinson, who caught the ball midstride as he was slashing unguarded though the key and gently laid the ball against the glass and into the net. The scoreboard flashed 2—0 for the home team.

The quick score stunned the Utes, who had barely stepped away from the center circle.

Doing his best to guard the lightning-fast Robinson, Sheff had two fouls by the end of the first quarter. Vadal sent Wat in to replace Sheff in an effort to contain Robinson and keep Sheff out of further foul trouble. As the teams took the floor to begin the second quarter, scattered boos flowed from the stands. Undaunted, Wat stayed in front of Robinson and did his best to shut down the former Globetrotter. Halftime arrived with the Utes trailing 33–27.

The Quartermasters controlled the tip to start the second half, but the Utes were prepared. Bob Lewis dropped back and intercepted the outlet pass to Robinson. Sheff was on his game and scored easily from the key in the third quarter, however he picked up two more fouls by the end of the period. Arnie, Wat and Herb continued the offensive attack, as Sheff watched the game from the bench to start the final quarter. Sensing the need to get his captain involved, Vadal sent Sheff back into the game with two minutes gone in the period. The well-conditioned Utes were outhustling the Fort Warren veterans, and with seven minutes left in the game they led 48–47.

They held the lead until the clock at the scorer's table showed three minutes remaining. Playing tight defense, Sheff slapped Robinson on the arm while defending a set shot and fouled out of the game. He walked silently to the bench with nineteen points while Vadal let loose a tirade at an oblivious armed services referee about the bad call. Despite the loss of their leading scorer, the Utes continued to battle evenly. But Rivlin scored the next nine points for Fort Warren, and the close game ended in favor of the home team, 61–59. Arnie played well, scoring sixteen points; Wat had ten and Herb totaled nine points for the game.

Following a short team meeting with Vadal and Pete, who praised the team's best effort yet, the 14–1 Utes silently showered and walked to the bus for the short ride back to the barrack. At the beginning of the season the team just wanted to play ball and have a good time; victories, if any, would be an unexpected plus. However, once victories started coming—especially against good opponents—the team's undefeated season became a rallying point for the youngsters. Their loss to Fort Warren was the first blemish on their perfect season.

The train left the Union Pacific station the next morning and would arrive in Salt Lake at 6:45 Wednesday morning. During the trip the players had time to catch up on missed homework, relax and—for Wat, Arnie and the Lewis brothers—play bridge. At 10:00 p.m. Vadal called for lights out and each player returned to his assigned berth for the remainder of the trip.

Arnie was quickly lulled to sleep by the rhythmic clacking of the huge metal wheels. A timid tapping on the folding door of his cramped resting space roused him from his sleep. He rolled over and squinted hard to see the luminous hands of his travel alarm that lay next to his pillow. It was 1:30 a.m. He fumbled in the dark, found the latch of the sliding door and pushed it open to find Wat standing in the hallway, pillow, blanket and clothes in hand.

The Union Pacific Railroad followed a firm policy, embraced by all railroads and bus lines during the war, giving priority to servicemen and servicewomen on all modes of public transportation. They could bump nonmilitary personnel if adequate accommodations were not otherwise available. On an early-morning stop in Rawlins, Wyoming, a sleepy army officer returning from leave boarded the train the Utes were traveling on to return to his post. He needed a berth for the remainder of the night, and the conductor, who had noted the name *Misaka* on the passenger list, unhesitatingly gave him Wat's. Wat apologized to Arnie for the intrusion and crawled onto the outer edge of the bunk. Arnie pressed his back against the window to make room for his friend and teammate.

After unpacking his bags from the road trip and having a quick lunch, Vadal read the mail while relaxing in an overstuffed chair in his living room. Near the center of the stack of bills and correspondence was a telegram from Kansas City, Missouri. Though Vadal noticed it immediately, he didn't open it until the rest of the stack had received his attention. At the beginning of the season he had just hoped to have a team to put on the floor, let alone one that would bring a sense of pride to the university. As the season progressed, his team developed and the wins stacked up; and locked away in the back of his mind was a thought he was afraid to entertain. He knew that the communication in his lap was an invitation to the NCAA Basketball Tournament, the upstart national championship tournament that was vying for attention with the more established and prestigious National Invitation Tournament. The Western Regionals were going to be held in Kansas City and the finals were to be played at Madison Square Garden in New York City near the end of March. For now Vadal would keep the invitation secret from his players. He was concerned that the distraction would cause his team to lose focus. They had six games left to play and three of them were against outstanding teams.

The sports reporters in Salt Lake excitedly wrote about the Utes, nicknaming them the "Blitz Kids." The moniker described the fast and furious defense they played and their unusual create-as-you-go offense, both of which were reminiscent of Germany's *blitzkrieg*, or "lightning war," that its army had used at the beginning of World War II. The choice of the nickname pleased Vadal; however he was more pleased with the fact that they hadn't used a name that had a more negative connotation, especially for his team, like the "Kamikaze Kids."

Following an easy win over a military team from nearby Kearns and a forty-seven-point blowout over a team of staff members from Bushnell Hospital, a military hospital in Brigham City, the Kids were scheduled to meet another basketball powerhouse on February 12. The Salt Lake Air Base Wings boasted a record of eighteen wins and only one loss, a two-point loss to Ecker Studio early in the season. The Wings were on a collision course with Fort Warren for the Service League Championship. Like Fort Warren they were loaded with talent.

Though Vadal was familiar with the Wings' lineup, he reread it one last time as he sat in his car before leaving for the Deseret Gym. Most of them had played at universities across the country. While Vadal's squad was a gaggle of underclassmen, the Wings were upperclassmen with time on the floor. Ed Ehlers was captain of the team and a former Purdue University star; guard Bob Cowan had played for Indiana University; starting center Ray Lumpp played for NYU; Bob Shaddock had been a starter at Syracuse University; and Rolph Fuhrman from the University of Oregon would start at forward.

The gym was packed with 3,000 fans as the teams took the floor to begin play. It was immediately obvious to the Blitz Kids why the Wings had won eighteen games: they were physically stronger than the skinny Utes. On the Wings' third possession, the Utes extended their defense and forced Cowan deep into the corner. Dick, who had picked him up as he crossed the top of the key, backed off his defense and challenged him to take the shot. The ball floated off Cowan's fingertips and sailed toward the basket. As it arched upward it hit the bottom of the running track fifteen feet short of the basket. With a loud thunk the ball fell to the floor. In anticipation of the dying duck, Herb jumped and plucked it out of the air on its first bounce and fired a pass to Sheff, who was already at half-court when the shot left Cowan's hands. Sheff gently laid the ball into the net before any of the defenders had a chance to get across the half-court line.

The Utes fought hard, but at halftime trailed the Wings 24–15. The second half didn't treat the Utes any better, as Eddie Ehlers took over for the Wings. He dominated play and ran roughshod over the Ute defense—the first time anyone had done so all season. At the final buzzer, the Wings had prevailed by a wide margin, 59–34. Ehlers scored twenty-five points for the Wings and Arnie had sixteen to lead the Utes.

Utah had three games remaining in their patchwork season. Their record was a glossy fifteen wins and two losses, and they had played some of the best amateur and semiprofessional teams in the country. Two of the remaining games were against teams who would be heavily favored to defeat the Utes. On February 26, Keith had scheduled Dow Chemical, an amateur team from Midland, Michigan, who traveled the country promoting Dow Chemical products and annihilating its opposition. The Dow team was led by two-time all-American Milo Komenich, a six-foot-seven-inch giant who had led the University of Wyoming Cowboys to the NCAA Championship the year before. Komenich had a supporting cast that was no less formidable, most notably John Buescher, a former all-conference forward/center from the University of Kansas. The Utes would close out their regular season on March 4 with a rematch against the Salt Lake Air Base Wings.

In arranging to rent the church-owned gym where the team had been playing its home games, Vadal understood that if there were a conflicting church function, the Utes would have to find another place to play. He hadn't given much thought to the potential problem at first. But as it turned out, the game against Dow Chemical would fall victim to a church dance festival. Arrangements were quickly made to play the game at a local high school gym—the Utes' third "home court" of the season.

To begin the game, Sheff outjumped Komenich, who towered over him by a full half foot. That set the tone for the Utes, who outhustled and outshot the Dow Chemical team for the first three quarters of the game. Vadal realized he could not match up against the height advantage that Dow held over the Utes, and decided to try to out-quick the team by playing Wat for most of the game instead of Dick. In spite of the Utes' quickness, however, Komenich dominated play in the key in the final ten minutes of the game. Utah, unable to stop his spin hook shot, ultimately lost by a score of 46–36.

Having lost two of their last three games, the team sat dejectedly in the small high school locker room. Vadal reminded them that they had just played one of the best teams in the country at any level and had led for three quarters of the game. They should hold their heads high. They had the opportunity to avenge their earlier loss to the Wings in less than a week. They needed to prepare for a hard week of practice, because there was nothing worse in sports than to lose the last game of the season.

Vadal walked into the locker room thirty minutes before their rematch with the Wings and called the team together for a pep talk. Being a man who thought that any communication between human beings should be completed in the fewest words possible, he simply said, "I want to have a meeting in the locker room after the game tonight. Now play hard and let's go out winners."

The Wings had battled through a hard-fought loss to Fort Warren just days earlier, during which Ed Ehlers had felt a twinge in his back. He played against the Utes, but he wasn't the overpowering force he had been in their previous meeting. As far as the Utes, it was as if the Wings were facing an entirely different squad than the one they'd dominated in their last meeting. The Blitz Kids shared the ball and were unafraid to wait to dish the ball until they found an opening. Wat was a wild man on defense, stealing several balls from the reeling Wings.

For the Utes, the scoring was as evenly balanced as it had been all year, with Sheff and Arnie each finishing with fourteen points, Herb and Bob with thirteen apiece, and Wat with seven. A desire for revenge had pushed them on, and the Utes played as well as they had all season. By the final buzzer, they were avenged to the tune of 62–38.

Following the game, Vadal, Pete and Keith walked into the locker room to the sound of Wat's towel snapping at Arnie while he stood under a hot shower. As Arnie grabbed a towel to counter Wat's assault, Vadal called the team together. The towel-clad Kids, anxious to leave the building to celebrate the end to a successful season, gathered around their granite-faced coach, who stood with his arms folded across his hulking chest.

Vadal said, "Boys, you have played hard all season, and I'm here to tell you that the season isn't over." He held up two telegrams. "We have a decision to make. We've been invited to play in both the NCAA Basketball Tournament Western Regionals in Kansas City and the National Invitation Tournament in New York City."

Team members stood with their mouths open upon hearing the news. They had read rumors of the possibility of their participation in one of the tournaments in the newspapers, but figured they were just that—rumors. There hadn't been even a mention of the possibility from the coaching staff.

Vadal put it to a vote to see which invitation they would accept. Arnie and Sheff were the only two who had been to New York, and most of the rest of the team hadn't even been out of the state of Utah. If the Utes accepted the bid to the NCAA Western Regionals in Kansas City and lost, their only option would be to pack their bags and go home. If they *won* the regionals they would go to New York for the NCAA finals, but winning two games in Kansas City would be a tough task. If they accepted the NIT bid they would go directly to New York and play in Madison Square Garden. Even if they lost early in the tournament the Kids could spend another day or so sightseeing before they returned to Utah. It might be the only opportunity most of the team members would have to see the Big Apple.

The vote was unanimous. They were going to New York, to the Garden, to play in the NIT.

BRIGHT LIGHTS OF
THE BIG APPLE

*If a tie is like kissing your sister, losing is like kissing your grandmother
with her teeth out.*

— GEORGE BRETT

Punching the horn two more times, Arnie stuck his head out the window of his car to see if Wat was coming. It was earlier than he was used to and he had hardly slept a wink the night before. The sun spilled into the valley from the mountains to the east, washing away the sepia tones of early morning and welcoming the bright greens of early March. But the scenery escaped Arnie as he drummed his fingers on the steering wheel and muttered to himself, "Come on, Wat. Hurry."

Looking at the dash he saw the gas gauge hovering just above empty, and shifted again in his seat. Arnie knew if he could just exit the parking lot and turn the corner before running out of gas he could coast all the way to the Union Pacific station, where the team was meeting prior to their departure for New York. He couldn't get gas as often now that he was living thirty miles away from his family's farm, so he had developed a technique to maximize every drop. The idea was simple. The university was at the top of a large hill, and with the right timing and a little luck he could turn the engine off and let the car coast all the way downhill to the railroad station. He only had to run a few stop signs.

Finally Wat bolted from the building, tossed his heavy bag in the back and they wheeled around to the street. At the top of the hill, Arnie turned the engine off and they bounced their way to the train station.

The Plymouth freewheeled into the closest parking stall and groaned to a stop. Arnie and Wat grabbed their duffel bags, stuffed full of all the items the two inexperienced travelers thought they would need. Packed tightly in the canvas satchels were their basketball shoes, jockstraps, toiletries and clothes. In addition, Wat had packed a number of heavy textbooks. Without the burden of books, Arnie's bag was significantly lighter; instead of texts for school he had packed several decks of playing cards.

The boosters had apparently noticed Arnie's increased scoring average and had taken to calling him the "Blond Bomber." He reveled in the moniker and hadn't had a haircut for six weeks prior to the trip. If he were going to be known for his hair, he was going to make it look good—or so he thought. It now dipped below his eyes, and he had developed a habit of whipping his head to the side to swing the hair out of his face. Arnie loved his full head of hair, but his teammates were less than fond of his new vanity.

As he had done prior to the trip to Colorado and Wyoming, Vadal insisted on meeting the boys in the lobby of the train station before they boarded. He had everyone unpack their bags and place their basketball shoes and jockstraps into an empty footlocker. Vadal repeated his tired mantra: "If you don't have shoes, you can't play." He ended by stating firmly, "And if you can't play, we can't win. So I'll be in charge of the shoes!"

The players, which included the starting five plus Wat, Fred Lewis, Jim Nance and T. Ray Kingston, were milling around in the passenger car, tucking bags and belongings into cubbyholes and staking claim to their seats. They were as excited about the trip to New York as they were about playing in the NIT. The East Coast press didn't give them much of a chance against the real college basketball powers in the country—those that played in the Midwest and the East. Some had even questioned the quality of the Utes' opponents, saying they had only played two or three college teams all season—subpar college teams at that. For the Utes' part, even if they didn't play well in the tournament, they still intended on having a good time in the city.

As the Kids settled in, waiting for the train to pull out of the station, Arnie found a seat and was shuffling a deck of cards on the table before him. He felt a pair of hands resting heavily on his shoulders, and Sheff said from behind him, "Hey Bomber, looks like your hair needs a little trim!" Arnie looked up from the cards to see Fred Lewis standing across the table holding a pair of tape scissors. The remainder of the team stood behind him grinning. He knew that it was no use to try to run or fight; it would be him against eight other kids determined to put an end to his fashion statement. With two players holding each of his arms and legs, they laid him in the aisle of the car as Fred took the scissors to his forelocks. Trying to feign a serious attitude at first, Arnie couldn't help but laugh as he looked in the mirror at the results. *I'll be able to concentrate on basketball while I'm in New York,* he thought, *because I sure won't attract any girls.*

The players' initial excitement and anticipation for the trip quickly gave way to tedium. The tall young men were confined to the cramped quarters of the railroad cars with New York more than three days away. They had pulled off their one good joke on Arnie before the train had even left the station. Now, after only an hour and a half on the train, they were restless.

The train clacked eastward along steel rails through the Midwest. Dick sat by himself next to a window where he watched the sun shining over endless green fields of corn that unrolled across the countryside. Taking a break from his studying, he began to grow sleepy.

For the second time in fifteen minutes, Richard Lavell Smuin found himself lying facedown in his family's backyard chicken coop in a heap of feathers and chicken dung. He brushed the feathers, matted with bits of white and green droppings, from his hair, nose and lips and said to himself, "Don't cross your legs, you idiot, don't cross your legs." Rays of honey-colored sunlight seeped through the warped boards in the coop and made it difficult for him to see the bird as he continued the hunt for his quarry.

The knowledge that he couldn't leave the coop until he had the gamecock in hand pushed him on. His father's words echoed in his mind: "If you have quick enough feet to catch a gamecock, you can defend anybody." Dick didn't really understand his dad's obsession with basketball and would have rather played baseball, but Lavell believed that basketball was the game of the future and he insisted that Dick work on fundamentals. After thirty-five minutes, Dick opened the door of the coop with a startled and tired gamecock in his bloody hands. His father, Lavell, took the bird from him and returned it to the coop with the other cocks. He put his arms around his son and pulled him close, helping him brush the feathers and chicken manure from his clothes.

Dick was the only child born to Lavell and Helen Smuin. Lavell had been a great athlete in his youth and was naturally drawn to basketball. He excelled in the sport in high school, and following graduation competed for some of the best AAU teams in the state of Utah. Helen was crowned by a mop of fiery red hair and went by the nickname "Ted." When Dick was one year old, the Smuins moved from Utah County to Magna, Utah, near the Kennecott Copper Mine. Kennecott Copper had an AAU team that was in need of the five-foot-ten-inch guard's quickness and shooting ability. Senior management at the mine understood how important a successful team was in creating a positive public image, so they did some creative hiring and found a spot in their workforce for Lavell's tenacious playmaking. Lavell worked hard at the mine, but the salary of a laborer—no matter how well he could shoot a basketball—was not sufficient to support even a family of three.

Cockfighting was a popular though frowned-upon pastime on the west side of the Salt Lake Valley in the early 1930s. Lavell despised the gambling and booze that accompanied the cockfights. The casual loss of life, even though it was just chickens, disturbed him even more. But the sport provided a way for him to meet his financial obligations. Cockfights need gamecocks, and Lavell raised some of the best around.

Under his father's coaching, Dick grew up playing most sports during their respective seasons, but he preferred baseball and dreamed of playing like Babe Ruth or Lou Gehrig. Though his father encouraged Dick to develop his skills in any sport in which he showed interest, he always promoted basketball as his sport of choice. In between seasons, Dick and his father worked on foot quickness and leg speed. Dick's hands and wrists were constantly cut and bruised from catching the wily gamecocks, but at least the face-plants in the chicken dung became a thing of the past.

Dick had a stellar athletic career at Cyprus High School, starring in both baseball and basketball. However, hailing from a family of humble financial resources, Dick was not planning on attending college. His intent was to follow his father's footsteps and work at the mine until he was old enough to volunteer for the military. Those plans changed one Friday evening when a stern-looking gentleman with a square and prominent jaw walked into the high school gym during a Cyprus High basketball game. Dick played a sensational game that night, leading his team to victory with game highs in points and rebounds. Immediately following the game the man introduced himself as Vadal Peterson and offered Dick a scholarship to play for the University of Utah.

Dick couldn't afford a car, but the opportunity to play ball and have his college education paid for was an offer too good to pass up. His home town of Magna was twenty miles from Salt Lake City. Each morning he would rise early enough to ride the train to Union Station in Salt Lake and hitch a ride or walk the three miles to the university campus. Following class and practice each evening, he would reverse the process, arriving home by 8:00 p.m.—leaving him just enough time to eat a late dinner, finish his homework and get to bed. As his friends and teammates could attest, Dick didn't have time for much of a social life.

The train rumbled eastward at a pace far too slow in the minds of the players. However, for Wat and Arnie it provided ample time to take advantage of Bob and Fred's poor bridge skills. For the first two nights of the trip the four card sharks squeezed into Bob's top berth, a space designed to hold one average-sized person. Packed tightly together, they spent three to four hours a night in intellectual combat. The mirrors on the ceiling of the train car were once again positioned perfectly for Arnie and Wat, with the unsuspecting Lewis brothers sitting with their backs to the mirrors. They let Bob and Fred win a few hands at first each night to set the hook. The competitive nature of the twins kept them in the game until they tired of the humiliation of constantly being beaten by their teammates.

The trip to New York was interrupted several times. Trains carrying enlisted men and wartime supplies were at the top of the railroad food chain, and all others had to give them the right-of-way. Several hours would pass as the players stared out the windows at the countryside waiting for the war to let them continue their journey.

By the second day the trip had become a practice in banality. There were only so many times Wat and Arnie could cheat their teammates before even that started to get a little boring. After countless stops and endless miles of cornfields, the team finally arrived in Chicago, where they had to travel several miles by cab to the New York Central Railroad station to transfer trains.

Vadal was so caught up in watching after his gang of juveniles that he neglected his duties as coach and caretaker of all things rubber. He had completely forgotten about the footlocker that contained their most precious cargo: their shoes and jockstraps.

While the team chugged their way toward New York, that one critical piece of luggage was on its way to Oklahoma. Vadal had been paranoid about the players losing their basketball shoes because he knew how hard they would be to replace, and jockstraps, with their elastic waistband and pouch, were also hard to find due to wartime rubber restrictions. Now he was responsible for losing every last one of them because he'd put the footlocker in the wrong place and forgotten about it.

The first thing Keith did upon arriving in New York was call sporting goods stores all over the city, but he wasn't surprised when none of the stores had jockstraps in stock or shoes big enough for the players. He then turned to other teams to see if there were another coach that might take pity on their plight. Before their first practice game, Keith had scraped together enough loaner shoes and jockstraps to cover all the starters and most of the reserves. "Treat them like your own children," Vadal told them, not wanting to accept responsibility for the lost footlocker. "If you lose them, not only will *I* kill you, but so will the kind player who saved you from playing in your slippers and long johns."

Everyone on the team was excited to be in America's biggest city, but their thoughts of competition in the NIT overshadowed any ideas of sightseeing. They were put up in the Belvedere Hotel across the street from the Garden, but they were not yet allowed inside basketball's mecca. All practices were scheduled at nearby gyms to accommodate the preparation for the tournament inside the arena.

The Utes' had a practice game scheduled against Oklahoma A&M, a team that featured one of college basketball's most enduring icons. In a time when height was not favored, seven-foot-tall Bob Kurland was almost a foot taller than most of his opponents. Kurland was so dominant that several rules were later adopted in an attempt to limit the effectiveness of him and his six-foot-ten-inch contemporary, George Mikan. Before Kurland and Mikan, no one had thought of putting their hand up through the bottom of the hoop and swatting shots away. Kurland did, and thus was born the rule against goaltending.

At the scrimmage, Vadal told Sheff, the shortest starter but highest jumper on the team, to guard the Okie giant. In spite of his amazing jumping ability, Sheff couldn't contain his taller foe. The two of them jumped for a rebound during the game, and on the way down Sheff landed awkwardly on Kurland's toes. His foot shifted in his borrowed shoe, rotating his ankle outward. The bone on the side of his foot hit the ground first, followed quickly by the rest of him.

Sheff limped to the bench, where Pete and Vadal tried to get him to relax. Pete pulled off Sheff's shoe to get a look at his foot. His ankle was already turning purple and swelling. The coaches talked for a minute before Pete ran off to find the tournament physician. Sheff grabbed his shoe and tried to slide his foot back in, but it was swollen too badly to fit. He sat for the rest of the scrimmage with his leg propped up on the bench and his ankle wrapped in a bag of ice, watching Wat buzz like a tiny mosquito around Kurland. The scrimmage ended on a similarly sour note. The teams hadn't kept score, but both knew Utah had come up short. Every member of the Utah squad left the scrimmage with a lingering fear of having to face Coach Hank Iba's team with their gargantuan center during the tournament.

Sheff made a point of walking back to the hotel on his own. He knew he would need to take it easy the rest of the night. Tomorrow was the first game of the tournament, but Sheff had a few plans of his own before then. He spent the entire morning in his hotel room with his leg propped up on a pillow. After noon, he donned a dress shirt and a skinny tie and limped out of the hotel toward the subway. While his mind should have been on the game, he was, after all, a young college man. An acquaintance back home had told him about a cute relative who lived in New York who wanted to meet the dashing ballplayer. So he went out into the big city, hobbling his way toward a blind date.

Vadal wanted to free his mind the day of their first game, so he chose to wander the streets and try to let the big buildings overshadow his concerns. He grabbed Keith for company and the two of them got a map from the front desk clerk. Looking the part of tourists, Keith and Vadal almost ran over a short man in a brown trench coat before they made it out of the lobby.

"You fellas coaches?" the man asked.

Vadal didn't know who was asking, but assumed he was a member of the press. So he gave his best grin and stuck out his hand toward the stranger, wanting to make a positive impression. "Yes, sir. Vadal Peterson, coach of the Runnin' Redskins from Utah. This is my graduate manager, Keith Brown."

Forcing a smile, the stranger shook both their hands. "Listen, I think I might be able to help you out. You'll be playing Kentucky, right? Have you seen any scouting reports?" He pointed to a large envelope in his hand.

In a time when basketball got little media attention, it was a nearly impossible task for coaches to learn about the teams they were going to play. Vadal knew about Kentucky's head coach, Adolph Rupp, who ultimately would become one of the legends of college basketball. As for the Wildcat players, he knew nothing. There were no television broadcasts to review and newspaper reports were not always reliable. Most of the time scouting reports were just a summary of the action from the first quarter of the game. Sometimes coaches got lucky and found people looking to make a buck by compiling reports on the different teams. This man appeared to be one such enterprising individual.

"Twenty-five bucks will give you a four-page rundown on the squad, with special emphasis on the starting five."

It was an offer that Vadal couldn't pass up. He ripped his wallet out of his pocket and dipped into his spending cash. This was the first time Vadal had laid his hands on a scouting report. He was so excited he felt like he was cheating.

After a quick read, Vadal decided on a drastic change in his defensive game plan. There was an apparent weak spot in the Kentucky squad—one that, if the Utes played it right, they could exploit to their advantage.

It was surprisingly quiet in the locker room before the team's first tournament game. Wat teased Arnie about his dapper new hairdo as they slid their bags under the benches. Sheff was whispering about how he almost didn't make it on time; he'd ended up in Queens after getting lost on the subway while trying to meet his blind date. He had limped around the subway tunnels for several hours before calling it quits and heading back toward the Garden. Behind their conversations was a low rumbling, almost like someone had started a stampede a few miles away.

Vadal's voice brought each of their conversations to a stop. "I'm not a man of many words. But I want you to know, before you go out there, that you deserve this. You don't realize it, but you've come a long way. Now go out there and give it all you've got. And if you do, win or lose, you'll still be champions."

"One last thing." Vadal seemed to notice the sound of the crowd, the stampede getting closer, and he raised his voice to compensate. "I know you boys aren't used to being around it, but people here will be smoking tonight. Try not to let it bother you."

He paused again, as if he were trying to remember something. "Oh yeah, the court is two inches higher than the floor, so if you step off the court, watch yourself. I don't want any of you falling on your face in front of all of New York."

He looked around as if expecting something from his players, and when they just stared back he tipped his head and said, "That's it, let's get out there."

Jogging down the cement tunnel in Madison Square Garden, each player felt like he was in a different world. Some were excited, others nervous, but none of them had any idea what they were in for. They were still just having a good time, giddy to be in the Big Apple.

A well of light thrown by two spotlights illuminated the space where the tunnel ended and the court began. The lights were so bright that the rest of the Garden was washed out in a darkness so thick it looked as if the team would be stepping into oblivion rather than onto a basketball court.

Vadal stopped in front of the players and brought them together in a huddle just before the light at the end of the tunnel. Leaning in, the Utes strained to hear their coach's words over the cacophony of the crowd. He put one arm on the shoulder of a player and pointed his other arm at the court just out of sight. They looked into the void as Vadal shouted at them, "Don't trip!"

One by one they ran out onto the court as their names were announced. They couldn't see anything, but the size of the crowd sounded gigantic. They felt odd waving to an invisible audience that roared with the voice of a giant.

Up until this moment the Utes had been playing a game. The tryouts, the season, the road trips—they were all exercises in fraternity. To the players, up until now basketball hadn't meant much more than having a good time and getting to see their names in the paper.

The lights in the Garden switched on and the enormous building burst into light. Taking a second to let his eyes adjust, Arnie swallowed hard when he looked up at the crowd. Row upon row was packed with men in suits smoking cigars and cigarettes. The assembly stretched up and up until it disappeared in a cloud of thick smoke. It looked as though all of New York City had crammed into one building that rose up into a nicotine-fueled heaven. The rumblings they had heard earlier resolved now into numberless shouts and the thundering of feet. The sound suddenly became overwhelming, almost painful.

In that moment, basketball ceased to be a game for the players from Utah; the fun was gone and terror had taken its place. The sound of 17,000 fans in the Garden sounded a wake-up call. The Deseret Gym was far, far away.

The Blitz Kids starters walked onto the Garden floor. Sheff limped badly to the center jump circle. His ankle was heavily taped and remained grossly swollen and the color of port wine. He could jump and run in a straight line without much trouble, but cutting and moving laterally, in addition to being painful, caused his ankle to shift and feel unstable. He downplayed the injury to Vadal and told him he could play, so the coach gave his team captain the chance to start.

The loud blast from the referee's whistle brought the teams into position at center court and silenced the titanic crowd. As the players jockeyed for position, Sheff and Wildcat center Bob Brannum crouched anticipating the ball toss. Jumping mainly on his good ankle, Sheff reached as far into the smoky air as he could, but was a good three inches short of Brannum's fingertips and the ball. For the first time all season, Sheff didn't control the tip; but more importantly, as he turned to run and defend the ball his foot slipped. After three minutes of hobbling up and down the court, it was obvious to Vadal that Sheff needed to come out of the game. He had scored three points, but he wasn't quick enough and he couldn't defend anybody.

Vadal looked down the bench at the reserves. With his team leader and top scorer unable to go, he had to make the right choice if the Utes had any chance against Kentucky. A thousand thoughts whipped through his mind as he assessed his players. In his mind, Wat was the best player he had in reserve and arguably deserved to be a starter. All season long he had kept him on the bench, not spitefully or because he harbored any prejudice himself, but because Wat was Japanese and the crowds all knew there was a war going on. With the biggest game of his coaching career on the line, Vadal knew he had no choice but to play Wat. He took several steps down the floor, placed his hand on top of Wat's head and asked, "You ever play center?"

The New York fans were well acquainted with the internment and general denigration of Japanese Americans that was occurring throughout the country. Now, here in their city, at their tournament, in their Garden, was a Jap running onto the floor. The crowd, not knowing how to respond, sat in silence as perhaps the first five-foot-seven-inch center in NIT history entered the game.

Wat didn't take the opportunity lightly. He had tried to decide throughout the season if his time spent on the bench was because he wasn't good enough, was too short, or had a name the coach couldn't stomach. That all faded when he stepped over the two-inch lip on the side of the court. The whistle blew and Wat was in his own world. He was born to play defense, and on that night he didn't give an inch to his opponents.

It became quickly apparent that the scouting report on Kentucky was a sham. Vadal, and the crowd, knew the game would probably be one-sided. Kentucky had already established itself as a team worthy of national attention, and the crowd seemed to be behind them. Utah, on the other hand, was thought to be a placeholder—someone for Kentucky to beat on their journey toward the later brackets. Vadal's one hope, that prized scouting report, had failed him. It identified Jack Parkinson as a great ball handler and playmaker but a poor shooter. Vadal had coached his team to back off their defense on Parkinson and double-team Brannum when the ball went into the post. Every time Kentucky brought the ball into the half-court the Utah defense collapsed on Brannum, while Parkinson bombed away from the outside, pushing the Wildcats to an early lead.

Herb called time-out and the Utes sat on the floor at the top of the key around the free throw line. The rules at the time prohibited the players from going to the bench during time-outs, so players on each team developed their own strategies without input from the coaches. The Kids decided to abandon the defense they had practiced and return to their familiar pickup man-to-man that had brought them to the Garden in the first place.

Herb and Arnie committed quietly to themselves to pick up the offensive intensity to make up for the hobbled Sheff, while Wat took the assignment from the team to shut down the high-scoring Parkinson. By halftime Utah had tied the score, 24–24. Wat's defensive intensity had impressed the New York crowd, and as the teams left the floor at intermission he received a polite applause from the fans.

The Blitz Kids brought an elevated level of intensity onto the floor at the start of the second half, and the crowd felt it. Arnie and Herb put the scoring burden squarely on their thin shoulders, and with Wat's defensive harassment of Parkinson, the Utes pulled ahead by seven points early in the third quarter. With the fans standing and cheering the efforts of this team of unknowns from Utah, Coach Rupp, fearing an early departure from the tournament, called a time-out hoping to stem the momentum that had swung Utah's way.

Suddenly for Arnie, Herb and the rest of the Utes, it was as if someone had turned off a switch. Shots that had been falling easily just moments earlier started rimming out. Free throws that had been slipping quietly through the net now looked more like large rocks thrown hard against a brick wall. The Wildcats pulled ahead.

Arnie saw an opening in the Wildcat defense and flashed unguarded across the key as Herb bounced a pass that landed firmly in the palms of his hands. He pivoted on his left foot and jumped to lay the ball off the backboard. As he jumped, he felt something familiar in his left knee: not a pain, but a shift. And then the joint locked up. As his shot dropped through the net, Arnie fell to the floor and his sweat-drenched skin squealed across the hardwood as he slid on his shoulder under the basket and off the court.

Unable to stand on his own, Arnie was assisted to the locker room by Keith and Pete. Sitting on the taping table, it was quickly apparent that he couldn't bear weight on his injured leg. Without Arnie in the lineup, the Utes had no chance of regaining the lead, winning the game and continuing on in the tournament.

Pete gently cradled Arnie's foot in his hands. With only rudimentary first-aid skills, he remembered a trick he had seen performed by a trainer years before. As Pete glanced at the door and said, "Hi, coach," Arnie turned his attention from his injured knee to the empty doorway. Just as Arnie turned his head, Pete gripped his foot firmly, slightly bent his knee and snapped his leg down hard. There was an audible pop from the knee. Arnie stared at Pete with a horrified expression on his face, anticipating the pain that was sure to accompany the loud pop. His expression quickly softened as he realized that the pain was gone and his knee could move freely.

After testing it for a few seconds, Arnie looked at Pete and Keith and blurted, "Let's go!"

Slowly, almost imperceptibly, the crowd began to shift its allegiance. At first there were a few cheers as Arnie trotted back onto the court. The Utes hustled to match the skill and grace of the Kentucky team. Wat was a human bouncing ball as he darted back and forth across the court to match every slightest move of his man, and the crowd took notice. But the Utes were overmatched and underskilled, and while Arnie had been in the locker room for five crucial minutes, Kentucky had extended their lead. The Utah players were putting their hearts on the line and fighting like this game meant everything to them. The fans in the Garden got caught up in the drama. The Utes continued to run full bore—even as their shots continued ricocheting off the backboards.

Utah maintained their intensity as the fourth quarter started. They outhustled, outrebounded and nearly outplayed the favored Wildcats, but it was as if fate had pulled an invisible lid over their basket. Even the stentorian crowd, who by now clearly favored the Utes, couldn't cheer away the tight grip that bad luck held over the Kids. In the end the fierce intensity the Utes brought to the Garden could not make up for a bad shooting night, and Kentucky claimed victory, 46–38.

Five physically exhausted and beaten kids from Utah walked off the Garden floor the evening of March 20, 1944, unmindful of the fact that though they'd lost the game they had won the acclaim of the New York fans and press.

A few hours after the game Vadal dragged Keith back onto the cold New York streets. He was still angry and Keith was one of the few people who could bear the brunt of his rants without wilting.

"There is nothing more crushing than hope that turns against you." Vadal shook his head and continued. "We traveled all this way with our heads in the clouds only to have them served back to us on a platter. You know, I spent the whole trip thinking about what it would be like to win? Silly! I actually let what those reporters have been saying get to me and ended up sitting in my berth all the way here thinking about winning a championship." It seemed as though he were talking more to himself now than to Keith. "I guess I wouldn't feel so bad if I hadn't started hoping."

Vadal's words hung in the air and Keith couldn't find a way to respond, so they walked a while listening to the sounds of the city. Mounds of snow framed the roads and sidewalks as they wandered. Undoubtedly people back home would ask them what New York was like, so they had set out to see the sights, but neither one noticed any of the lights above their heads.

Keith watched as block after block of sidewalk flowed under his feet. His mind, however, was still back on the bench in the Garden. He saw something out of the corner of his eye, which snapped him out of his hypnotic walk: it was a black shape nestled in the white snow. Keith bent down to grab whatever it was sticking up from the snowbank. As he pulled it up toward his face, he wiped the clumps of ice from his newfound treasure. Two gold-leafed words stood out on a black cover.

"It's a Bible," Vadal noted over Keith's shoulder.

In an instant, a childlike joy spread over Keith's face. Vadal's eyes rolled back in his head.

"Whaddya know!" Keith cheered. "It's a sign, Vadal. I heard it's good luck to find a Bible!"

"Sure, it's a sign someone's wandering around Manhattan lookin' for his Bible." Vadal was walking again, but now he was headed back for the hotel. It was about time this day ended.

Running after him, Keith didn't relent. "No, no, it means something! Just you wait; something good is going to happen!"

Vadal didn't have to respond; his face told it all. But he answered anyway: "Don't get your hopes up."

That night Arnie went to bed early. His knee was a bit sore but he had full motion. He had a hard time falling asleep as he poured over the details of the game in his mind. Losing didn't bother him so much; what really made him mad was how poorly they had played. The whole season had been building up to this game. It didn't seem right for it to be over already. He didn't want to admit it, but they were responsible for the loss. He couldn't chalk it up to the superiority of Adolph Rupp's squad, even though they were possibly the best team they had faced. The Utes had lost because they were a mess. They weren't the same team who had defeated the Salt Lake Air Base Wings or battled Fort Warren evenly right up until the end. Maybe it was the city, or the Garden. Whatever it was, against Kentucky they'd been a team of scared farm boys—exactly what the papers predicted they would be. Just a bunch of kids from nowhere.

Now it was over. It had been fun, but they had little to show for it. In the end it almost didn't seem worth it to travel so far only to lose their first game. They had traveled all this way to win, not to see Lady Liberty or the Empire State Building. That was what drove them: an insatiable thirst for the fast break, the feel of the leather as the ball spun in the palms of their hands, the cough of the net as the ball dropped through. They didn't care about accolades or titles, they just loved the mystique of five guys becoming one. Those moments when Wat knew what Arnie was going to do before he even thought about doing it, when everything else faded away and they could make magic happen. That night nothing had faded away. The lights were too bright, the crowd too loud, and the basket too small.

The ache in Arnie's heart wasn't unlike the injustice he'd felt when he was cut from his ninth-grade team. If only they had another chance, he knew they could beat anybody.

That same night as Arnie lay sleepless in New York, hundreds of miles away in Arkansas a team of doctors prepared to amputate the leg of another basketball player. Both boys lay awake, lamenting their misfortune. But as one player was watching his dreams turn to ashes, the dreams of the other player would soon rise from those ashes like a phoenix.

Arnie and the rest of the Utes were going to get their second chance.

FILLING IN

A wise man will make more opportunities than he finds.

— FRANCIS BACON

"We won't win, Keith. We learned that the hard way." Vadal's harsh voice was amplified by the look on his face.

"Maybe you're right, but we have to let them decide. It's their season."

"Right, if losing in New York isn't bad enough, why don't we hop another train, waste two days in transit, and lose another one in Kansas City. That sounds like a swell idea!"

Vadal stopped pacing, suppressed his sarcasm and continued. "They've never been to New York before, and might never again. Let them have some fun before they go off to war."

Keith, standing in his bathrobe, hugged himself and shuffled his feet. It was after 3:00 a.m. Almost an hour had passed since they had received the wire from the NCAA. Short on details, the telegram read:

University of Arkansas unable to participate in tournament due to accident. Team needed. First game on Fri. 24th in Kansas City. Arrangements have been made for hotel stay Thurs. evening. Will you play?

Drooping forward, Vadal shook his head and said, "Fine, go wake them up."

Rousing the boys was easier than Keith had expected. Most of them were still awake, talking quietly in their rooms. They all gathered around Vadal's bed. He was waiting, arms folded, until every player had found a place to sit or stand.

"We've got a decision to make." His tired eyes peered out from under his massive brow. "I know you thought your season was over, but we just received a telegram from the NCAA." Already Vadal could tell this conversation wasn't headed where he wanted it to go. The players' faces lit up as soon as he mentioned the NCAA.

"The team from Arkansas was in some kind of accident, and now the tournament needs someone to fill the spot; and as it turns out, we are the most available."

Arnie was sitting on Vadal's bed with a grin as white as his hair. He nodded disbelievingly and slapped Dick's knee.

"Boys, now, we could go, but that means we need to get on a train in a couple of hours. That means no sightseeing, no tour of the *Queen Mary,* no Times Square, none of the stuff we had planned to do while we're here. If you want to stay, we've got till the end of the week to have fun and live it up in New York before we have to go home." He paused before continuing. "Now, if we go to Kansas City and lose, the trip will be over. I don't think they have arrangements for us longer than the one night. We'll have to head back home. I know for several of you this might be your only chance to see the city before you report for military service. I won't blame you if you just want to pass on the offer."

"Hey coach?" Arnie asked. "Are all the games going to be in Kansas City?"

"No, they have the championship game here in the Garden. The winner of the NCAA Tournament also plays the winner of the NIT two nights later in a Red Cross benefit game."

Arnie's Cheshire grin grew even bigger than before. "Well, we came to play basketball, didn't we? I'm in favor of going to Kansas City. Then we'll come back here." It made so much sense to him, and as Vadal witnessed, every other head in the room nodded with approval. He knew he had been overruled.

Vadal didn't understand it, but for the boys it wasn't about the city or the sights. It was all about a ball and a hoop. All they wanted was an opportunity to get back to the Garden and redeem themselves. They knew that those thousands of voices that cheered for them against Kentucky hadn't been wrong. There was something different about this team, something that they weren't ready to let go of.

To the players it was simple. As bizarre as it was, they had the second chance that maybe they didn't deserve. Not only did they have the chance to come back to the Garden, but maybe they would also have the chance to take on the winner of the tournament that they'd just been knocked out of. It was an irony too sweet for them to pass up.

Vadal could have saved himself the time of asking the boys to vote: not one of them voted to stay in New York. Both Pete and Keith cast votes to go to Kansas City also, though Vadal didn't think they should count.

"Fine, if that's what you want to do you should probably go get packed. You can catch up on sleep once we're on the train."

Two days and two nights of late-night bridge games passed before the Utes arrived in Kansas City. It was late when they walked into the hotel lobby. The nervous hotel clerk cleared his throat and explained the situation.

"The folks who arranged for your room are expecting other people to arrive after you leave tomorrow."

Arnie looked at Keith and asked rhetorically, "Leave? Tomorrow?"

The clerk continued, "They also instructed me to ask you not to unpack your things because, technically, these rooms are reserved for those other folks."

Keith leaned toward Arnie and explained, "They think we're going to lose and didn't bother getting rooms for us after the first game."

Reacting at first with a sour expression, a grin sneaked onto

Arnie's face. "Well, well. I'm afraid that they're going to be very disappointed."

One by one, the rumpled and tired players climbed down the steps of the bus and into the side door of the Kansas City Auditorium. The auditorium was large by Deseret Gym standards, but pocket-sized compared to the Garden in New York. The Missouri Tigers were an all-civilian team—along with Utah, one of only a handful of such teams in the country. They had been a last-minute replacement for the University of Iowa, who had been forced to withdraw from the NCAA Tournament when three starters received draft notices and were required to report for duty. A reporter at the *New York Herald Tribune* summed up his expectations for the team from Utah with the caption, "Utah's Blitz Kids are just a bunch of string bean youths." The bookmakers had figured Missouri to be an easy eight-point favorite over Utah.

The Tigers couldn't have known what they were coming up against. They knew that the Utes had just come from a brutal loss against Kentucky in the NIT. They knew they were filling in for Arkansas, and how travel-weary the Utes would be. But what they didn't know was how the cheers of the New York crowds were still ringing in the ears of the Utah crew. The game in the Garden had started a fire that the Tigers' best efforts would not be able to put out.

For the second game in a row, Sheff doddered around on his sprained ankle during warm-ups. Vadal again gave him the nod to start the game, hoping that his diminutive center would provide the leadership the young Utes needed. Sheff easily outjumped Missouri's Jim Pippin to start the game, but he'd only played a little more than four minutes when he felt his taped ankle begin to swell and his foot go numb. The last thing he wanted to do was leave a game for the second time in less than a week, but he just couldn't compete. It was obvious to him, Vadal and everyone watching the game. The Tigers had taken advantage of his lack of speed and had run up a 12–7 lead. He wanted to play, but he wanted to win the game more. With only four minutes and thirty seconds gone in the first quarter, Sheff limped to the bench. Wat stood, took off his warm-ups and waited for the ref to motion him into the game.

As he entered the game, boos rang out and someone in the crowd shouted, "This ain't a Jap's game!" Wat didn't hear a word of it; he was in his own world. There was an immediate change in tempo as Wat batted away passes, stole balls and disrupted the Tigers' offense. The Utes roared back and led 27–14 by halftime.

Early in the second half the Blitz Kids extended their lead to twenty points, outpacing the Tigers 34–14. Vadal, realizing his team would play again the next evening if they won, substituted freely for the remainder of the game. Clearing the bench, he gave his other three substitutes a rare chance to play. The game ended with Utah winning by a score of 45–35. Arnie led all scorers with twelve points, followed by Herb with eight.

Earlier that evening Iowa State had defeated Pepperdine College to move into the Western Regional championship game against Utah. The game would be played the following evening at the auditorium, with the winner advancing to the NCAA finals on Tuesday, March 28 at Madison Square Garden in New York City.

The Iowa State Cyclones were champions of the Big Six Conference and had played some of the best college teams in the Midwest. They had a team that was filled in large part by navy seamen who had been seasoned college players prior to their military service. Utah slipped comfortably into its role as underdog going into the game.

Before the game, Vadal struggled with the decision to let Sheff jump center at the start of the game and the beginning of the second half. Sheff's ankle had become more swollen and painful during the short time he had played the night before. A full night of ice and elevation hadn't helped much. In the end the coach relented, but knew he would substitute Wat as soon as he could get him in the game.

Utah led by four points by the time Wat reported to the scorer's table. Scattered boos reminded the Kids that there was still a war going on with American lives being lost. In the view of many, the only good Jap was one who was locked up somewhere behind fences. Arnie stood with his hands on his hips shaking his head in disgust at the outpouring of hate while Wat trotted onto the floor. Wat, as usual, was seemingly unaware of the display. He clapped his hands and encouraged his teammates.

The spectators in the stands were not the only narrow-minded people in the auditorium that evening. Another was dressed in a black-and-white-striped shirt and had a whistle draped around his neck. The first time Wat received the ball in the frontcourt he was quickly called for traveling, although his feet were firmly planted on the floor in preparation for a set shot. Not two minutes later, as Dick was defending Iowa State's Price Brookfield, a whistle blew. Dick cautiously raised his hand, not wanting to admit the obvious foul he'd committed, but the ref pointed past Dick to Wat—who was nowhere near the action and a good four feet away from his own man. Vadal erupted from his place on the bench in protest of the preposterous call, but was firmly warned by the referee that any more outbursts would be countered with a technical foul.

Wat had a certain pride in his game. He stuck to his defenders like pine sap, but he never racked up a lot of fouls and had never fouled out of a game since he started playing at Central Junior High. That perfect record ended against the Cyclones. Early in the fourth quarter he picked up his fifth foul—the victim of suspect calls rather than overaggressive play. Vadal was desperate to hold on to the lead, so he gritted his teeth and sent Sheff back in. He was limited to moving slowly and deliberately, but he had better court sense than anyone else on the bench.

Sheff kept close to the basket and labored for each shot—but they went in. The Blitz Kids picked up their passing game and were quick in cutting to the basket. They held on until the final buzzer, and earned a 40–31 victory. Wat and Sheff, after four quarters of playing musical chairs, led the team with nine points each.

Earlier in the evening Dartmouth College had defeated Ohio State to win the NCAA Eastern Regionals at Madison Square Garden. Sunday, at the same Garden location, St. John's University would beat George Mikan and the DePaul University Blue Demons to win the National Invitation Tournament Championship.

It wasn't really a smile that made a brief appearance on Vadal's face that evening at the team dinner—more of a half-smile perhaps. It was the first hint of satisfaction the team had seen all year from their stoic coach.

Fred spoke up. "Come on coach. You have to admit it. It was right to come to Kansas City."

The half-smile returned for an instant and Vadal said, "You'll have two days on the train to rest before we get back to New York, so everybody in bed by midnight."

Arnie and Wat arrived back at the hotel at 11:45 p.m. and were in bed by the appointed hour, but since news of the Eastern Regionals championship had not yet reached Kansas City, they didn't know who they would play for the NCAA title. The two lay in the dark discussing whether they would play Dartmouth or Ohio State and the advantages of playing one or the other. Before sleep found them, the sun rose on Sunday, March 26.

Vadal knew that these kids would get themselves lost if he blinked too long, so he kept them on a short leash as they made their way to the train station Sunday morning. He was the last person into the fourth taxi, not letting any of the cabbies leave until he made sure he wasn't missing any players. Once at the station, Bob, excited to return to New York, rushed out of the cab without looking back. It wasn't until they found their train and were about to board that Bob realized his mistake. The train tickets to New York were in a briefcase that Keith had asked him to carry and guard with his life, a briefcase that was now traveling around the city in a yellow cab. The boys had seen Vadal angry many times during the season, but this time his face was such a bright shade of red it looked as though his head were expanding. The madder he got, the bigger his head seemed.

"Nice, Bob. Real nice work!" Vadal exploded. "I'm glad I've got such a bunch of smart kids on my team, because otherwise I might have to brush your teeth and dress you in the morning. How could you, Bob? How could you?"

Vadal droned on and on. He had conveniently forgotten his own similar mistake with the footlocker just a few days earlier. The whole team was eager to find the tickets, primarily to stop Vadal's rebuke. A few minutes before their train pulled out of the station, and just before Vadal's eyes popped out of his skull, a short cabbie appeared out of the massive crowd, briefcase in hand.

"You guys weren't too tough to find. I just had to ask if anyone had seen a bunch of string beans walking around the station. Some old lady led me right to you."

The team climbed aboard as the train doors were closing, but it took Vadal several hours to simmer down. Thinking about the up-coming game with Dartmouth further hampered his sleep. He lay in his berth that evening thinking about their game in the Garden.

The Big Green of Dartmouth College in Hanover, New Hampshire, were an excellent team. Coach Earl Brown's roster was loaded with veteran players, many of whom called the New York area home. Coach Brown and his players figured playing in the Garden against a team from the West would be like playing on their home court with 15,000 fans in the stands cheering them on to a lopsided victory. Dartmouth College was one of the schools whose basketball team had been bol-stered by the Navy V-12 Program. They had lost several of their sub-stitutes to the draft, but picked up some outstanding talent through the V-12 Program. Captain Aud Brindley, a six-foot-four-inch center who had scored twenty-eight points for the Green against Ohio State in the Eastern Regionals, was one of the few on the squad who wasn't part of the V-12 Program. Aud would lead the tournament in scoring, averaging 17.3 points per game. After military service, he would play pro ball for the New York Knicks during the 1946–47 season. The Green also added Cornell star freshman Bob Gale, who would return to Cornell following his military service, and after an outstanding col-lege career would be the seventh overall pick in the BAA draft in 1947. The most notable addition for Dartmouth was Dick McGuire. Dick played sixteen games of the 1943–44 season with St. John's University, then joined the Dartmouth College V-12 Program in time to play the last five games for the Green, and was named a Helms Foundation all-American after the tournament. Following his service to the country, Dick would return to St. John's and continue his collegiate basketball career. He was drafted by the New York Knicks in 1949 and played for them until 1957, when he was traded to the Detroit Pistons. He finished his pro career with the Pistons in 1960. He led the Knicks to three NBA finals, was a seven-time NBA all-star and was elected to the Basketball Hall of Fame in 1993.

Since Dartmouth's team was made up primarily of servicemen whose first obligation was to defend the country, getting time off from military service to play in the tournament was difficult. The players had just enough leave remaining to play in the championship game against the Utes, and no more. The team and supporters would have to leave New York the next day and return to Hanover.

The Utes clambered off the train after the two-day trip from Kansas City in the same rumpled clothes they had worn when they'd left Salt Lake City fifteen days earlier. They were a group of players, mostly freshmen, with little previous college experience. Their sophomore center had a badly sprained ankle, and his replacement was a five-foot-seven-inch Japanese American whose total playing time prior to the Iowa State game didn't add up to one full game of basketball.

One New York sportswriter wrote, "If you look up the word *underdog* in the dictionary, you would see a picture of the University of Utah basketball team standing on the railroad platform in Kansas City looking for their tickets."

THE BLITZ

A basketball team is like the five fingers on your hand. If you can get them all together, you have a fist.

— MIKE KRZYZEWSKI

The Dartmouth team could taste the National Championship. The Big Green had been to the NCAA Tournament each of the three previous years but had yet to bring home a championship. In 1942 they made it to the finals but lost to Stanford, 53–38. They had a 20–1 record going into the game with Utah, their only blemish being a 44–30 early-season loss to an air force team from Mitchell Field on Long Island, New York. The New York press had already proclaimed them the best team in the nation. Tom Meany, a legendary sportswriter for the *New York Star* and *Collier's* magazine, provided the headline, "Whad'a Know! They Play Basketball in Utah."

If the Big Green players lacked anything, it was not confidence. Their conversations focused on how they would trounce the team of string beans from Utah who looked so frail that if they sneezed too hard they would break. They figured the Blitz Kids had just been lucky to get this far in the tournament. Dartmouth had seen the Utah–Kentucky game and had witnessed Utah's poor shooting that night and assumed it was a typical performance for the Utes. They chuckled about number 22, the lanky kid who had hair that looked like it had been cut with a lawn mower, and wondered how anyone would let him out of the house looking that bad. To a player, they figured that the tough Dartmouth defense would have little trouble shutting down the Utes' top scorer. The tournament title was theirs for the taking, like a flower in a garden just waiting to be picked.

On Tuesday evening, an hour and a half before the start of the championship game, the Utes clustered together in their locker room. Pete was taping Sheff's swollen ankle, while Arnie, Wat, Dick, Herb, Bob and the three other subs sat in close quarters. Herb was walking around the room encouraging his teammates, but his audience was lost in their own thoughts.

Vadal entered the locker room, gathered his players together and said, "I've talked to the Ohio State coach, who told me that we need to guard Brindley and Gale and we can back off the defense on Vancisin. So as we run our pickup defense, I'd like Herb to pick up Brindley each time you can. Dick, I want you on Gale, and Lewis, drift away from Vancisin when the ball goes into the key and help Herb and Dick shut down the middle." Then with a wry smile he said, "I didn't have to pay for this scouting report, so maybe it's good information. But if it works like our defense against Kentucky, then go back to our regular pickup man-to-man; it's what got us here."

The coach then admonished them: "Tonight as you are introduced before the game, remember that all the lights in the arena will be off and it will be black out there. We'll stand at the end of the tunnel. When your name is called, the spotlight will shine on you and you'll dribble the ball to the jump circle. When the spotlight goes off roll the ball back to the next man waiting in the tunnel, and he'll do the same thing until you are all on the floor. And remember the lip on the floor. I don't want anyone tripping and getting hurt; we'll run out of players."

After everything they had been through, it surprised Vadal that these boys still didn't seem to realize what they were up against. Their demeanor defied their circumstances. By the way they were talking and preparing, it was as if they were just getting ready to trot out into the Deseret Gym for another game, not as if the NCAA Championship were theirs to grasp. The thrill of the night wasn't in the possibility of the championship that baited them. It wasn't the almost tangible tension in the air; it wasn't the crowd and it wasn't even the Garden. They had overcome their fears and were no longer blinded by the competition. They were driven by something internal, something no one could have foreseen. They were furiously intent on beating the snot out of anyone who dared step onto the court with them, and it didn't matter who it was. They would play with all the passion they could muster.

There is a certain comfort in ignorance. The fact that the Utes didn't fathom how much of an underdog they were protected them from their own doubts. They couldn't understand the role they would play in the history of the game. If they did, it would have crushed them. They could not have known that the following few hours would change the course of their lives forever. If they would have known, they never could have accomplished the task before them. They would have folded under the pressure.

Vadal felt helpless, knowing that he would have to spend the game outside the boundaries of play, watching them—these kids, his kids—make all the decisions for the most important game Vadal had ever been a part of. His role would be minimal. Come halftime, he knew his advice would be old news: techniques they had picked up earlier in the game, inspiration they had no need of hearing. Vadal knew that, for the first time, they didn't need him. His greatest contribution would be as their supporter and cheerleader, not as their leader. In spite of their youth and appearance, they had surpassed him.

The Garden was nearly filled with close to 15,000 faceless suit coats with ties and full-length dresses with hats. That number, however, was several thousand less than a capacity crowd for Madison Square Garden. Ned Irish, the basketball promoter for the most famous sports arena in the world, knew that the reason for the lower-than-expected ticket sales was that most basketball fans in New York felt the game would be a runaway victory for the Green. He could have sold more tickets if two first-rate teams were playing, but fate had teamed the Green against a bottom-bracket understudy. People were buying tickets, but they weren't standing in line for them.

Being a businessman, Irish was disappointed with the news that should Dartmouth win the championship, they wouldn't be able to fill the spot in the Red Cross benefit game against NIT champ St. John's because of their military commitments. Utah had been invited to play in the benefit game whether they won or lost tonight. He knew that a game featuring two great East Coast teams would be a sellout. The prospects of Utah losing to Dartmouth and then playing St. John's as a second-place team would be a financial disaster, both for the Garden and the Red Cross. Though he wouldn't admit it to anyone, he was pulling for the Utes to win tonight.

Standing in the void between the tunnel and the court, the Utah team huddled together again. Another well of light blazed in front of them, awaiting their return to the Garden floor. The atmosphere was the same as they had experienced not too long ago: the thunderous cheer of thousands of fans, the choking smell of the thick smoke-filled air, the boom of the announcer's voice. The Garden was the same—just as threatening as before—but they were different.

With the intense light blinding his eyes, Sheff heard the public address announcer broadcast, ". . . and for the University of Utah, Fred Sheffield." He couldn't see more than eight inches into the black abyss of the darkened Garden as he dribbled the ball toward where he thought the center of the court was. He knew there was a two-inch trap jutting up from the subfloor in the basketball court, waiting to reach up and grab his toes if he weren't careful. Luckily he made it safely to center court and turned to face where he thought his team-mates waited at the head of the tunnel. Just then the spotlight went off. He carefully rolled the ball back in what he guessed to be the direction of the tunnel as the announcer boomed the name "Dick Smuin." The spotlight pierced the darkness to find Dick on his hands and knees searching under some chairs for the ball. Fortunately for Dick, someone just outside the illuminated circle handed him a ball and he took his turn. As each player heard his name called, he stepped into the blackness, hoping the circle of light would follow and guide him to center court.

There was a significantly louder roar of approval from the fans when the Utah team was introduced than when the Big Green took the floor. Arnie made a subconscious note of the crowd's response, a point he thought was odd, but which he didn't really give much thought to at the time. He had read in the New York papers that they had won over the hearts of the fans in their hard-fought loss to Kentucky. But he assumed that against an East Coast team he and his teammates would be looked on as the enemy, especially considering that, in the minds of some, one of the Utes *was* the enemy.

Sheff hobbled onto the floor for the jump ball, followed by the remainder of the starters. He had only lost one tip to start a game the entire season, and that was in the loss to Kentucky. He wasn't superstitious, but he wanted to make sure the Utes had the first chance on offense. It was Sheffield at six foot one against Brindley at six foot four. As the ref tossed the ball in the air, it was obvious who wanted it most: Sheff's hand reached higher than Brindley's. From the bench, it seemed to Vadal for just a second that Sheff had jumped so high his head and shoulders had disappeared into the smoky haze that hovered above the court. There was scattered applause from the fans as Utah gained control and took possession of the ball.

Arnie took the ball and dribbled into the frontcourt. He bounced the ball to Bob, who was standing just to the right of the key. He lofted the first shot of the game from fifteen feet, and it bounced hard off the front of the rim and high into the air. The rebound was battled for and controlled by Herb, who banked in a shot from under the basket. Utah took the lead as the fans stood and shouted their approval.

Dartmouth's play was intense and focused, as their well-prescribed offense and man-to-man defense challenged the Utes at every turn. However, the road-weary Kids responded with their unorthodox, no-set-play offense and an emotional defensive effort that shocked the Dartmouth team and coaches. They had seen from the newspaper box scores that Herb had played every minute of the last five games, and Arnie had played all but the few minutes he'd spent in the locker room with his knee injury during the Kentucky game. The Green figured to wear them down with hustle and overtake them in the end.

With the score still 2–0 after several more possessions, Dartmouth brought the ball inbounds. Brindley caught Arnie standing flat-footed on defense. He drove the ball around him and laid a gentle shot off the glass to tie the game at 2–2.

For the first few times up and down the court, Sheff felt like his ankle would hold up; however, the tape was becoming tighter and he slowly felt the ankle beginning to throb with pain. Vadal noticed his limp, which was more pronounced, and he began to question Sheff's ability to stay in front of his player while on defense. At the first opportunity Vadal called timeout and took Wat by the sleeve of his warm-up, telling him to go in for Sheff. Sheff limped off the court and sat at the end of the bench, hands covering his weeping eyes, as Pete, for the fourth game in a row, wrapped a bag of ice to his ankle long before the battle was over.

The New York crowd apparently remembered Wat for his fly-in-your-face effort against Kentucky and stood to applaud as he entered the game. Arnie made an underhanded layup and was fouled hard; a successful free throw put Utah up 7–2. The Green scored the next two baskets. An inside shot by Brindley off a missed layup and a twenty-five-foot set shot by Dick McGuire that dropped straight through the cords brought the score to within one at 7–6.

Finding themselves behind to what they considered an inferior team, Dartmouth battled every second the ball was in play, but the Utes didn't give an inch. Every move Dartmouth made was met by passion from the Kids; hustle was met by emotional fury. The Ute bench stood and cheered their outmanned and overlooked team. A hook shot by Arnie brought the score to 17–16 for the team from the West, but a final shot by Gale just before half put the favored Green in the lead at the break by a score of 18–17.

At halftime, Vadal stood in the locker room before his players without a thing to say. These "Blitz Babies," as one reporter had called them, had just led the best team in the nation for almost all but the last few seconds of the first half. Vadal knew his team was tired; they hadn't slept in their own beds or had a home-cooked meal for almost two weeks. They had spent every ounce of effort they were able to reach down and find in their hearts and laid it all out on the floor. He knew that the five players who had finished the first half would have to go the rest of the distance if they had any chance of winning. He only hoped that their skinny legs would carry them long enough to meet the task. In his best fatherly voice he said, "Boys, there is nothing more I can tell you or anything I can say to inspire you. Let's go out there and do the same thing for the next twenty minutes and see what happens."

As the team walked onto the floor to begin the second half, Vadal looked at his bench. He had only four players sitting in reserve, and one of them couldn't play. He looked at the Dartmouth bench; they had eight players ready to fill in for one of their starters. He chuckled and shook his head, remembering the first practice of the year and the comment he had made to himself: "I should'a been a math teacher." And here he was with these eggheads, his string-bean team, in a dog-fight for the NCAA Championship.

Sheff's ankle was so badly swollen that he couldn't jump center to begin the second half, so Bob timidly stepped into the jump circle. The referee tossed the ball in the air and the tip was controlled by Joseph Vancisin for Dartmouth, but the Green promptly threw the ball out of bounds. Wat inbounded the ball to Arnie, who dribbled up court and tossed up a shot from the free throw line. He charged the board to get the rebound from his missed shot and made an easy layup from under the basket.

Following two easy Dartmouth buckets by Brindley and Gale, Dartmouth edged back into the lead. Arnie stepped up his offense, scoring on a drive to the basket from the left. Herb and Bob continued to sag into the middle to cover Dartmouth's big men, trying to stifle their offensive threat.

Arnie and Herb were feeling the burning thighs and calves of too many minutes played in too many games in too few days, but ignored their aches and pushed on. Arnie took a wild set shot from deep in the corner that would have bounced off the bottom of the running track in the Deseret Gym, but he had found his rhythm and the shot popped the cords as the ball floated through the hoop. Utah took the lead, 24–22.

As the second half wore on, the physically spent Utes continued to summon every bit of strength and endurance they could muster. Leading 34–30, the weary boys from Utah called a time-out. While the Dartmouth players sat in a circle diagramming plays on the floor, the Utes took the opportunity to just sit and rest. They didn't call any special offensive plays because they didn't use any, and the defense seemed to be working fine.

With thirty seconds left in the game and a lead of 36–34, Utah controlled the ball and was running the clock down. They could sense an upset in the making. The faceless suits and dresses in the nearly packed Garden were standing and chanting in unison, "U-tah, U-tah." All the Kids had to do was let the air out of the ball and sweet victory would be theirs. They would be national champions.

But a poor pass from Wat to Dick bounced into the stands, and in an instant Dartmouth had been given a reprieve. They inbounded the ball. Vancisin took the ball into the frontcourt, well defended by Dick. Sensing a draining game clock, he passed the ball to McGuire, who with five seconds left heaved up a running hook shot from thirty feet. Like an arrow, it bounced off the glass and into the basket to tie the game. The clock on the scorer's table read 00:00. The Utah–Dartmouth game would be the first overtime game in NCAA Tournament history.

The Dartmouth bench erupted, along with the fans who had trav-eled with the team from New Hampshire. The Green players sprinted to the coach's side, and he immediately started to outline plays for the extra period. The Utes gathered at center court and walked off the floor together to a thunderous ovation from the spectators, who now considered themselves Blitz Kids fans. Each of the Kids stood bent at the waist, hands resting on his knees, head bowed, listening to Vadal say, "I don't know how you can have anything left to give, but if you do, give it now." They weren't as worried about having strength enough to play as much as they were about having the strength to just walk back onto the court to begin the overtime period.

After a two-minute break, the Ute players stood around Bob as he once again faced Aud Brindley at the center jump circle. With the toss of the ball Wat stepped in front of McGuire. The ball was tipped in their direction and Wat snatched the ball from McGuire's hands. He quickly passed the ball to Arnie. Slashing to the basket, Arnie picked up his dribble in front of Brindley, spun . . . and dragged his pivot foot. The ball was turned over to the Green on the traveling call. Playing tight defense, Dick slapped Vancisin on the arm, which put him on the free throw line for two shots. He made the first shot from the line, which gave the Green a 37–36 lead, but missed the second shot.

On the next possession Wat inbounded the ball. Arnie brought it into the frontcourt and passed to Herb, who returned the pass. Arnie was fouled hard while driving to the hoop from the right of the lane and fell to the floor. He had scored eighteen points in regulation to lead all scorers. Now he stood at the free throw line with two more points waiting for him. Sweat from his brow dripped into his eyes. As the ref handed him the ball, he wiped the sting away from his eyes with his soaked jersey. He toed the line and calmly dropped both shots through the net, pushing Utah into the lead by one and increasing his game total to twenty. A single free throw by Brindley tied the score again at 38–38.

The crowd was standing and cheering on their adopted sons. The Utes willed their leaden legs to work, but they were spent. With the score tied 40–40 and twenty-five seconds left in overtime, Wat gathered in a long rebound and passed the ball to Bob standing on the right of the key. He knew there was little time left, but from his position he couldn't see the clock. He set his feet, thinking about a shot, but the defense by Gale was too tight. Out of the corner of his eye he saw Herb standing undefended three feet from the top of the key. With a prayer he hurled the ball in Herb's direction and watched as he caught the pass. Herb hesitated just a moment, then took half a step backward to square himself with the basket.

The hoarse fans in the Garden fell silent as Herb raised the ball over his head. The defenders were too slow in getting to him. The clock ticked down to three seconds as he looked up. There it was; a clear shot at the basket. He lofted the shot as flashbulbs in the stands exploded and camera shutters snapped. The soft leather ball took flight and arched toward its goal. The ball bounced softly off the iron rim, careened from the back of the iron to the front of the rim and bounced three more times. As if enjoying the moment, the ball paused before it finally rolled through the net.

Two seconds remained on the clock, just enough time for Dartmouth's McGuire to grab the ball off the inbounds pass and hurl it toward the far end of the court. But there were to be no more second chances for the Green. The shot sailed past the backboard and landed in the mass of screaming fans as the clock finally came to rest at 00:00.

Still in another world, Herb and the rest of the Kids were hunched over, ready to pounce back into action. Then the sounds of the crowd began to register in the ears of the players. The Big Green players walked off the court and stood on the sideline, watching the Utes stand in a stupor for several seconds, not knowing what to do, not quite ready for the game to be over. And then, as if on cue, Utah's three substitutes sprinted onto the court, knocking Arnie and Herb to the floor. As unbelievable as it was, Vadal cracked. A smile spread so far across his face he bore little resemblance to the harsh man they all knew. His incredulity betrayed his stoic sensibilities. Sheff limped to join the fray along with Vadal. Pete and Keith walked slowly, dreamlike, onto the court as the players lifted Herb into the air. They shouted and hugged each other, reeling in disbelief. NCAA officials rushed on the court to round up the team for photos of the new champions with their trophy.

In their excitement, Wat and Arnie had grabbed the wrong warm-up jackets, and they paraded around the court with each other's number and name across their backs. They were just two boys, both who had lost a parent and found themselves playing a simple game. They came from different, unequal worlds in the same hometown. In a war-torn and fear-filled country, one had faced a hateful world. But basketball had made them equals. So much so that Arnie didn't even notice the ends of his sleeves hugging his forearms, and Wat was unaware of his sliding down over his wrists.

Arnie and the rest of the team hadn't treated Wat with some sort of superficial racial sensitivity or kindness for the sake of charity. He was simply one of the team. By the way they treated him, he never sensed that he was any different.

Many on the team had played an important role in bringing them to this point: Sheff's jump balls, Arnie's scoring blitz, Herb's game-winning shot. And while Wat was a fitting symbol of the team as a whole—disregarded and unexpected—in a way he was wholly different. He was so unaware of others' doubts that he wasn't affected by them. He had won the hearts of the New York crowd, and they cheered as loudly for him as for anyone else.

For the first time in NCAA history, the reporters and tournament officials named a freshman as the Most Outstanding Player. For his stunning 22 points, more than half the team's total, Arnie wholeheartedly deserved the award. The next time a freshman would receive this honor would be more than forty years later, and in the history of college basketball there have been only two others to receive the award as freshmen: Pervis Ellison in 1986 and Carmelo Anthony in 2003.

The Utah locker room following the game was chaotic, filled with reporters anxious for exclusive interviews with Vadal, Arnie, Herb and Wat. Cameras flashed and relentless reporters took notes as the Blitz Kids mugged for photos and relayed their personal stories of the game. Holding the championship trophy aloft, Vadal walked among the crowd rubbing the trophy on the top of each of his players' heads, telling them, "You boys won this, every one of you won this."

Hundreds of miles away in a small Arkansas town, a battered group of basketball players had gathered around a radio in a small Fayetteville kitchen to listen to the game. Bound together by fate, they listened to the kids who were there in their place. They cheered for the team from Utah they had never met, and as they cheered they winced at their still fresh wounds—wounds that would never heal.

Fate had taken a moment in time and set the Utes on the road to a championship—a road they would ride for the rest of their lives.

REDEMPTION

Everybody pulls for David, nobody roots for Goliath.

—WILT CHAMBERLAIN

The Utes were feeling flush and nearly blew their budget at Jack Dempsey's Restaurant, where they went to celebrate their win after the championship game. Returning to the hotel after dinner, they sat in the lobby reliving the game and talking about the winning shot when Vadal, still with a rare smile on his face, sat down and reminded them that their season wasn't over. They still had the benefit game to play against NIT champion St. John's University. With that, their celebration was over; Vadal expected them all to be in bed in thirty minutes.

Arnie, Wat, Fred and Bob took the first elevator to the tenth floor, where Wat and Arnie shared a room next to Vadal and Pete. Herb, Sheff, Dick, Jim Nance, and T. Ray Kingston waited for the next elevator. As the door opened and the boys started to enter, three young ladies stepped inside as well. Jim, being a handsome but shy young man, smiled at the staring admirers. One of the girls giggled and said with a not-so-innocent voice colored with a Bronx accent, "Aren't you the basketball team from Utah?" In unison, the five turned and looked down at the trio. One of them handed Jim a folded piece of paper and said, "Here's our room number. You can come over later if you'd like." Immediately five jaws dropped open and ten eyes stared at the paper in Jim's hand, but no one could utter a word. As the car reached the tenth floor, the door opened and the Kids stepped out as one of the young ladies quipped from the back of the car, "It's obvious that the only thing you guys know how to play is basketball."

Sleep didn't come easily for the Utah contingent. Some thought of the championship game they had just won, replaying highlights in their minds. Others were thinking of the game to come.

Long after they should have been sleeping, Arnie pulled down the covers of his bed and sat on the edge with his feet on the floor.

"It doesn't seem real, does it?" he said. "If we win tomorrow night, we'll be the best team in the country."

Using the best imitation Western drawl he could muster, Wat responded, "Not bad for a bunch of hicks from Utaaaaah." They both laughed long and hard.

Around midnight Arnie heard a loud banging through the thin walls that separated their room from the hallway and Coach Peterson's room. He sat up and strained to listen to the ruckus in the hallway. He heard Vadal talking.

"Who are you? Don't you know what time it is?"

A gruff voice, thick with a New York accent, barked back, "I represent some big money and we want to know what it would take for you to go easy in the game on Thursday."

Arnie leapt out of bed and opened the door to the hall just enough to look out and see Vadal grab the man by the lapels of his coat and toss him against the wall across the hallway. The stranger bounced off the wall and fell to the floor.

"Don't bother coming back!" Vadal yelled.

He slammed the door, then reopened it and added, "And you stay away from my boys!"

Baseball had its problems with gambling, and there were rumors that point shaving was making its way into college basketball. Vadal had dedicated his life to the sport and didn't want anyone changing what he thought was a beautiful game.

With his typical pessimism, Vadal was concerned about an emotional letdown. His kids had just won the NCAA Championship and still hadn't come down to earth by Wednesday evening, just twenty-four hours before their game against St. John's. They'd had a light workout at an athletic club Wednesday afternoon and seemed loose but a little too playful. He had hoped they would be focused on the next game and completely embrace the opportunity that lay before them.

St. John's had been a good team during the regular season, but not stellar. They had won the NIT in 1943 and had a tradition of great teams. However, they had been an eighth seed going into the NIT in 1944 and weren't favored to advance beyond the first round. During the tournament they reached the potential many had expected to see earlier in the year. They had defeated Kentucky and a heavily favored DePaul University team that boasted future Hall of Famer George Mikan. Joe Lapchick, the coach of the Redmen, was a legend in college basketball coaching circles. *New York Post* correspondent Arch Murray wrote in the March 30 sports section, "Actually, St. John's shouldn't have too much trouble in this one. Lapchick, who has only to look at a team once to spot its flaws and loopholes, did a thorough scouting job on the westerners Tuesday. He was wearing a smug smile as he departed into the night."

St. John's University was located in Brooklyn, and five of the players on the team were from New York City. The Redmen truly had a home-court advantage over the Utes playing in Madison Square Garden. The game was being billed as a matchup between Most Outstanding Player award–winners for the NCAA and National Invitation tournaments: Arnie Ferrin for the Utes and Bill Kotsores for the Redmen.

The Red Cross had been the beneficiary of $35,000 in 1943 from the receipts of the Red Cross benefit game. This year the sell-out crowd of 18,125 paying fans would net the Red Cross in excess of $45,000 from the Utes–Redmen game.

Vadal stood in front of the team before the game, and in a no-nonsense style that was prototypical Vadal, simply said, "Boys, this is a good team. I hope you're ready. Now, let's get out there and beat 'em."

He could see in their eyes that the playfulness was gone and the competitive spirit had returned. He had seen similar spirit and competitive fire only occasionally with previous teams and in previous seasons, and it usually came from well-seasoned senior players. This year that spirit was evident in each of the young players who had fallen into his lap. He played only five or six players each game as a rule, and yet night after night they ignored fatigue and willed their bodies to compete when there was no more fuel left in the tank. They had out-hustled and outplayed nearly every team they faced. As they left the locker room and walked into the tunnel that led to the Garden floor, Vadal raised his eyes and whispered, "Please, just one more time."

Being the local favorite, the Redmen received a rousing welcome from the New York fans as they entered the arena; the Utes received a gratuitous applause as they started their warm-ups. On the sidelines, Vadal again noticed something he'd grown accustomed to during the season: Arnie, probably his most physical specimen, was six foot four and weighed a relatively meager 155 pounds, while all of the St. John's players looked as quick and muscular as halfbacks. It was as if his tall but underdeveloped boys were playing mature men. The contrast of the Kids success with their appearance had never stopped being a source of amazement to the veteran coach.

Sheff stepped into the center jump circle to face Ivy Summer, the Redmen center, who at six foot eight stood seven inches taller than Sheff. Although still hobbled by a sprained ankle, the springs he had for legs boosted him high enough to easily control the game's opening tip.

Utah failed to score on the first possession of the game, while the Redmen scored on a two-handed set shot from the top of the key by Hy Gotkin. After trading ends of the floor four or five times without a score, Arnie launched a left-handed shot from twenty-five feet that popped the cords. He was fouled on the shot by Kotsores, who was play-ing tight defense. Arnie made the free throw, putting the Utes up 3–2.

The lead for the Kids was short-lived, however, as the well-executed offense of the Redmen allowed for some easy baskets. St. John's scored on a give and go and several backdoor plays, feeding the ball to Gotkin and Ray Wertis for open layups under the basket.

Sheff left the game for good after the first seven minutes because of his ankle. He was replaced by Wat, who brought his usual tenacity to the floor. Though Wat was not the natural athlete Sheff was, his speed made the difference in the Utes' defense. More than anyone else on the team, Wat played with a style that bordered on mania. He was like a snake coiled to strike. When the Redmen least expected it, he would lash out, stealing the ball from their hands.

Whereas the Redmen were refined and polished, the Utes were ferocious and ungainly. The Utah crew were nowhere near as experienced as their opponents, and it was readily apparent to anyone watching the game. But the Utes played as if it really mattered. They never held back. They put everything they had into every pass, every shot. They leapt for every loose ball as if it were made of glass and only they could keep it from shattering on the floor. While the Redmen struggled to keep their composure, the Utes struggled to keep themselves from running wild.

Arnie launched a long set shot with his right hand that found its target, but two quick baskets by St. John's pushed them ahead 13–10. They extended their lead to 16–10 before the Utes shored up their pickup man-to-man defense and began to shut down the Redmen. Utah tied the game at 19–19 on baskets by Arnie, Herb and Wat in the closing minutes of the first half.

Momentum was swinging in the Utes' favor, and the crowd stood and cheered the underdogs from the West as they exited the floor at halftime. The change in fan support surprised the sportswriters, who had tabbed hometown St. John's as the overwhelming crowd favorite.

Showing their youthful exuberance, the Utes were in position thirty seconds before St. John's took the floor to begin the second half. They stood waiting before the fickle New York crowd, who were quickly becoming believers in the Blitz Kids.

Bob stepped into the circle to jump against Summer. Summer timed his jump poorly, allowing Bob to control the ball. Utah missed their first scoring opportunity of the second half and the Redmen took control. They brought the ball into the frontcourt and ran a figure-eight weave at the top of the key until Gotkin was free under the basket. He finally got open for a pass but missed an easy shot.

The Utes and Redmen played evenly for the first seven minutes of the second half, keeping the score within one or two points. As play continued, the tenacious Utah defense began to take a toll on St. John's. The crowd cheered every defensive play Wat made, and the pickup man-to-man began to confuse the Redmen. The Kids started picking off passes, and the same shots that St. John's had been sinking easily in the first half started bouncing off the rim, a sign of tired legs.

A left-handed set shot by Arnie put Utah in the lead by a score of 28–23, which was stretched to 33–26 with some outstanding shooting from Herb and Bob. Wat continued his ball-hawking defense and his superb passing to open players, and the Utes continued to outshoot and outdefend the Redmen. The conclusion of the game had become seemingly inevitable.

There was nothing the Redmen could do to stop the Utes. It didn't matter that the beanpoles from Utah had spent most of the last three weeks on trains since they left Salt Lake City, and had slept in a different room nearly every night. What they lacked in polish they made up for with determination and wild abandon. As the game ebbed away, the Redmen didn't break from their proper approach to the game; the Utes, on the other hand, flew at every opportunity as if the game depended on it.

With time on the clock draining away and the score 43–36 in favor of the Utes, Arnie brought the ball across the half-court line. The Kids passed the ball from one side of the court to the other two or three times to run down the clock before the ball came back to Arnie. He dribbled the ball toward the center circle and stopped. With two seconds left in the game, he heaved the ball far up into the thick Garden air. By the time the ball touched the hardwood again, the game had ended and the Blitz Kids were, beyond doubt, the best college basketball team in the nation.

The Utes were immediately enveloped by reporters and well-wishers. Mostly all they could do was laugh; they had no idea how else to deal with the situation. Everything in the Garden descended into a blissful chaos as people scrambled to get a look at the boys from Utah who had climbed to the top of the world. Nothing could be heard above the cheers and guffaws of the crowd. In some ways that noise is still ringing in the ears of the players today.

Having celebrated their NCAA Championship in the Garden just two days earlier, the team decided to return to the hotel quickly following the game. There they dined on fruit salad and met with several Utahans living in the City. Later in the evening they were guests of a group of University of Utah alumni at the Copacabana nightclub. On Friday, Vadal had his wishes realized when the Utes rode the Staten Island Ferry and toured the city. They were entertained at a dinner hosted by CBS and attended a performance of the stage show *Mexican Hayride* as guests of Ned Irish. They ended their sightseeing and celebrating by appearing as guests on *The Kate Smith Hour,* where they were introduced to the radio audience as national champions.

The team boarded the train on Sunday morning, heading home for Salt Lake. In all, the Utes had spent twenty days on the road—including eleven nights spent sleeping on trains—in their unlikely pursuit of the collegiate basketball crown. The president of the Denver & Rio Grande Railroad was so excited to have the team riding home on his train that he placed them in his personal car for the trip between Denver and Salt Lake City—the only stretch on the entire route that the team, and especially Wat, didn't have to worry about getting bumped from a berth by military personnel.

The team was greeted upon their arrival in Salt Lake at 7:00 a.m. Tuesday morning by thousands of cheering fans. The players were loaded into the backs of half a dozen convertibles and paraded with horns honking throughout the city. The team was scheduled for celebratory dinners every night for two weeks as the guests of nearly every local civic and social group. Tournament game films were shown throughout the state to ardent fans who packed sold-out theaters to see the games.

As unexpected as the Blitz Kids' National Championship seemed to the public, the unlikelihood of the team's feat was inadvertently underscored in the March 30 edition of the University of Utah's newspaper, the *Chronicle.* The entire front page of the paper was devoted to April Fools' Day stories about the school's faculty and staff, written to bait the unsuspecting reader—stories so ridiculous no one would believe them, such as "Polygamy Cult Discovered at U." Across the bottom of the front page, in large type, the very last sentence read, "Utes Defeat Dartmouth for National Hoop Championship, see story on Page Four." Most readers who had not heard the broadcasts of the games thought the story was so outlandish that it was just another joke perpetrated by the *Chronicle*'s editorial staff.

Basketball fans across the country were stunned by this group of youngsters, but no one was as surprised as the players themselves. They started out as a group of unproven underclassmen who just wanted to play ball. In the end they had caught the attention of a nation struggling to believe in itself, and for a brief moment gave that nation something to cheer about.

Sports have captured the imagination of America for years. There is something special about the way we invest our hearts and hopes in the games of children. The challenges that our heroes face on the court or field remind us of the greatness that we strain to achieve in our own lives. Seeing minor victories helps us to have hope for our own potential, as we consider that we, too, might be as those mythologized over time.

These young boys that didn't belong captivated the nation because they were willing to overcome odds they didn't understand. They accomplished the impossible because they didn't know that they weren't supposed to. They had a love of the game and a drive to excel, and no one's preconceived notions of their supposed abilities or lack thereof would stop them.

The thousands of people in Madison Square Garden forgot that they were supposed to cheer for the hometown team and got caught up in the drama that reflected their own lives. Instead of cheering for the team that was supposed to win, they cheered for the one willing to defy the odds. Instead of cheering for the favored and refined players, they couldn't help but root for the substitute center who barely stood over five and a half feet tall; the boy who was so focused on his role that he didn't have time to think about the many times he had been passed over because of his race. Getting the ball to the man who could score permeated Wat's mind, and he didn't have time to entertain the thought that no one other than his teammates and himself believed he could do it.

We all like to think that deep down inside of us there is the potential to accomplish great things if only the opportunity were to present itself. Here, with this game of basketball, played by those who were barely more than children, just such an opportunity had arisen. As this epic lesson played out in front of the sell-out crowd, one might envision that the tough New York fans saw in their own lives the same battles that were being fought on the court. They were hoping that the Utes would prove to them that greatness was possible, that the impossible could happen. If this ragtag bunch of kids could beat the best teams in the nation, then perhaps they, too, were giants just waiting for the chance to grow.

THE BEGINNING

How far you go in life depends on your being tender with the young, compassionate with the aged, sympathetic with the striving, and tolerant of the weak and strong—because some day in life you will have been all of these.

— GEORGE WASHINGTON CARVER

Every great sports story continues on after the championship game, as the players grow older and live their lives. This story is no exception. For the 1944 University of Utah Utes, their NCAA Tournament victory was only the beginning, a stepping-stone for the rest of their lives. Someone once said that success breeds success, and the lives of each of the Blitz Kids is a perfect application of that principle. Though none of the Utes see the 1944 season as the crowning moment of their lives, they all delight in the fact that they were a part of it.

The tale of the 1944 NCAA Tournament is not complete without the tragic turn of events that ended the season for the University of Arkansas. Just as the championship was a springboard for the boys from Utah, the deadly accident outside Fayetteville also had a lasting effect on the lives of those who were involved.

George Kok is the only surviving member of the 1944 Arkansas team. He was named all-conference every year for the remainder of his time at the University of Arkansas. He led the conference in scoring for two years, and held the record as the school's all-time leading scorer for thirty years after his collegiate career ended. He had a short stint in semiprofessional basketball, but eventually settled in Louisville, Kentucky, working as a high school athletic director. Now retired, he lives with his wife in Louisville.

Coach Lambert and the Razorbacks made it to the NCAA Tournament in 1945 and finished in a tie for third place. Lambert later coached at Memphis State and the University of Alabama before becoming the athletic director at Memphis State. Four of his teams made it to the NCAA Tournament, and he lived to see the University of Arkansas win the NCAA Championship in 1994.

Mike Schumchyk went on to become a successful engineer, but he was haunted by the 1944 accident. He was the only uninjured player in the car, but he never forgot the sights and sounds of that night. The thought of his teammates lying in the road that fateful night was something he thought about every March when the NCAA Tournament would come around again. Following the accident, he continued his athletic career at Arkansas, eventually graduating and playing professional football briefly with the Los Angeles Rams in 1946. He spent most of his career as an engineer in Arkansas.

Following the accident, Ben Jones and Deno Nichols, the two boys who were seriously injured, developed a strong bond. Deno had been transferred to another hospital, but the two sent letters of support to one another. They talked about their pain, but still had the youthful spirit to joke about the food at the hospital as well. After numerous surgeries, Ben eventually overcame his injuries and walked out of the hospital on crutches—in spite of his doctors urging him to use a wheelchair. Deno, however, never got over his injuries.

Ben was married to his girlfriend, Inez, in a bedside ceremony while he was still in the hospital. The two talked about their future, and planned for what their lives together would be like after he was able to walk again. Ben didn't allow the tragedy of that night to dictate the rest of his life. He coached both high school basketball and football in Arkansas, with some of his teams even winning championships. He continued on as a high school principal and superintendent. He dedicated himself to public education and never stopped looking forward. He died in 1984 of a heart attack shortly after spending Christmas Day with his children.

Deno's wife Virginia stayed at his bedside most of the time he was in the hospital. She could sense Deno was dying inside. He initially cancelled all his plans for the future and tried drowning himself in alcohol. He eventually found some success, but felt cheated and saw the accident as the cause of all the unhappiness in his life. Even years after the accident, Virginia would find him weeping at night, holding the stump where his leg used to be. Deno held several jobs and even coached a very successful swimming team, but he and Virginia eventually separated after he took up drinking again. The last time Virginia saw Deno was a few months before he died. She was quoted in the *Charlotte Observer* as saying, "He was in a wheelchair. There were big circles under his eyes. He looked like a shrunken old man. He wound up in the hospital and refused to eat. They tried to feed him intravenously, but he'd yank the needles out. I believe he wanted to die."

Maurice Russell, the driver of the other vehicle, died in 1984. He never contacted any member of the Arkansas team, and the reasons for the crash that night remain a mystery to this day.

The lives of the University of Arkansas players who were involved in the accident stand in stark contrast to the lives of the Utes.

One could argue that, in wartime America, basketball was lacking in real talent and the '44 Utes just happened to rise above the mediocrity. In fact, at the beginning of the 1944–45 season, the Utes met St. John's again in an exhibition match. With most of the '44 Utes now serving in the military, St. John's cruised to an easy victory. But in 1947, by which time Wat, Arnie and Dick had all returned from the war, the Utes defied the odds again, putting together another brilliant season. They returned to Madison Square Garden to seek redemption in the NIT. In the championship game, Utah beat Adolph Rupp's Kentucky squad—the same team that had crushed their hopes three years earlier.

There can be no doubt the Utes deserved every accolade they received. But in a way they were a fluke—not in their luck, but in the serendipitous collection of talent that came together in the fall of 1943. They all appeared at the same time, on the same team, exactly when it turned out they needed each other so much. They were just a bunch of Utah bumpkins, with only one bona fide recruit (Dick Smuin) among them—a bunch of homegrown boys who had innocently signed up on a list for basketball tryouts because they just wanted to play the game. Arguably, no Utah team has brought so much natural talent to the floor in one season, and certainly no Utes team since has achieved what they did. Alone, each of the boys would have been a great addition to whatever team they played on. Together they made history.

Vadal Peterson continued coaching basketball at the University of Utah, and in 1947 guided the Utes to the NIT Championship in a return visit to Madison Square Garden. He retired following the 1953 season after twenty-six years as head coach at the university.

Vadal had a reputation as a calloused and dispassionate individual who demanded the very most from his players. However, in spite of his tough exterior, he had a kind and compassionate core. Following his retirement, one of his former players who had just taken a position at a high school in Salt Lake teaching and coaching basketball became seriously ill and was admitted to the hospital for an extended period. School district policy mandated that the pay for a substitute teacher filling in for a full-time teacher be deducted from the full-time teacher's salary—money that the young man with his new family could not afford. Quietly and without being asked, Vadal volunteered to step in for his former player, teaching his classes and coaching the basketball team without pay. When the teacher was released from the hospital weeks later, he was stunned to find he had a full paycheck waiting for him.

Vadal died in September 1976 at the age of eighty-four. His career coaching record at the University of Utah included 385 wins and 230 losses, for a winning percentage of .626. Those 385 wins are still more than any other basketball coach in the university's history.

Dick Smuin was ordered to report for military duty the same day the team returned home from New York in early April 1944. The

Department of the Navy granted Dick a one-day deferment to report for active duty, which allowed him to take part in the Utes' championship celebration.

Following basic training, he was assigned to the light cruiser *Biloxi* and served in the Pacific theater. While cruising toward Japan to provide support for the Allies' eventual occupation, the *Biloxi* came under fire by Japanese Zeros. Dick was seated at his station four floors below the deck when a bomb struck the ship and penetrated deep into its body. It came to rest within a few feet of Dick but failed to detonate. The *Biloxi* continued on its course, and Dick spent the rest of his active duty in Nagasaki.

Following the war he returned to Utah, where Vadal had a position waiting for him on the Utes' 1946–47 basketball team that would go on to win the NIT Championship. He continued his college career over the next two years, and graduated with a degree in physical education and coaching.

After graduation, the Philadelphia Warriors offered Dick an opportunity to play pro ball. So Dick and his wife Joan, with their new baby boy, packed their car with their belongings and moved to New Jersey. He played for the Warriors during the preseason before team management encouraged him to work on his game while playing for the minor league Utica Pros of the American Basketball League. Leaving his family in Philly, Dick moved to upstate New York to continue to pursue his dream of a professional basketball career. But the Smuins found that supporting two households on the East Coast on the salary of a minor league basketball player was too difficult, so at the end of the season Dick decided to move with his family back to Utah.

Since he had survived the war in spite of the Japanese military's best effort to blow him up, he decided to try to have a positive impact in the lives of young men who might follow in his footsteps. He took a basketball head coaching position at Granger High School near Salt Lake City, while competing with the Meadow Gold Dairy AAU team satisfied Dick's need to continue playing ball. He held the coaching job at Granger High for five years before returning to Magna and assuming the same position at his alma mater, Cyprus High, where he had learned the game himself.

After an illustrious career, Dick retired from coaching in 1976.

In order to stay involved with the game he loved, he volunteered as an unpaid coach for the sophomore basketball team at Cottonwood High School in Murray, Utah. He died in September 2001 of complications from renal failure, just seven months after the death of his wife, Joan. To honor his legacy at Cyprus High, the school annually honors its most outstanding basketball player with the coveted Dick Smuin Award.

Herb Wilkinson received a deferment from military service to study dentistry after transferring to the University of Iowa following his freshman year at Utah. At Iowa, Herb played basketball and participated in track and field for the Hawkeyes. He was named all-Big Ten and all-American three times in basketball and was the Big Ten high-jump champion. After graduating, he declined an offer to play pro ball with the St. Louis Bombers in order to continue working toward a degree in dentistry.

Herb spent another year at Iowa taking graduate classes in anesthesiology in anticipation of completing a fellowship in oral surgery. Being a devout Mormon, he had always planned on serving a two-year mission for his church, and the span of time between his graduate study in anesthesiology and his fellowship in oral surgery seemed like the ideal time to fulfill his goal.

While Herb was looking for something to do to earn money to help support himself during his upcoming mission in England, the Minneapolis Lakers were gearing up for preseason play. The Lakers, it turns out, were in need of a big guard to fill out their team roster. Arnie, who had been drafted by the Lakers after graduating from Utah in 1948, phoned Herb and asked him if he were interested in filling the spot on the Lakers roster. John Kundla, coach of the Lakers, followed Arnie's phone call with one of his own and offered Herb the position. Kundla granted Herb's request not to play on Sundays out of respect for his religious beliefs, something Herb felt so strongly about that it would have been a deal breaker if the Lakers had forced the issue.

Herb reported to Minneapolis and joined the Lakers just in time for their first preseason game. He played in all of the preseason contests, and although he didn't start, he shot well and was a great defender—just what the Lakers needed. Coach Kundla was pleased with his new guard and felt that the Lakers could do without Herb for the few Sunday games that were on the schedule. However, just before regular-season play started, the owner of the team asked Coach Kundla why Herb wasn't on the bench for a Sunday home game against the Bombers. The coach's explanation seemed simple enough, but the owner would have no part of it. Herb would either be a Laker for every game or he wouldn't be a Laker at all. Being true to his convictions, the decision was easy for Herb: he said good-bye to Arnie and the rest of the team, and his short-lived pro career was over.

Following his missionary service, Herb returned to Iowa and completed a two-year oral surgery fellowship. He planned to return to the West to practice his profession, and considered opportunities in Utah and Arizona before accepting an offer in Los Altos, California. He practiced oral surgery for forty years before retiring.

Herb and his wife have five children. After retirement, the Wilkinsons moved to Southern California, where they lived for several years before returning to Utah. Though now in his eighties, Herb continues to participate in sports at an elite level and competes in track and field events at four or five senior games each year. He trains three or four days per week and competes in the high jump, long jump, shot put, discus, javelin and standing long jump. He is the current world record holder for his age class in several events.

Fred Sheffield followed up his 1943 NCAA high-jump championship and the Utes' 1944 NCAA Basketball Championship with continued success in track and field for the University of Utah. He garnered a second-place finish in the 1944 NCAA Track and Field Championships in the high jump; first and third place in the high jump and long jump, respectively, at the 1945 championships; and second place in the high jump in 1946. Upon graduation no less than seven professional basketball teams contacted Fred and offered him contracts to sign with them. No doubt they recognized his almost limitless natural athletic ability.

However, Fred had been accepted to medical school at Temple University in Philadelphia, so he turned all but one offer down. Eddie Gottlieb of the Philadelphia Warriors offered him a one-year contract that allowed him to play only home games and not have to travel with the team on the road. He signed the contract, which allowed him to devote his time during the week to being a medical student and still let him play the game he loved on nights and weekends to make some money.

After graduating from medical school, Fred completed a residency in physical medicine and rehabilitation. He was given a commission and entered the army as a medical officer. He enjoyed the military, and soon decided that with his specialty in rehabilitation he could provide a great service to the injured solders who returned to the United States with spinal cord injuries, head injuries, amputations and other disabilities. Fred decided to make the army his career, eventually achieving the rank of colonel.

He held positions as chief of physical medicine and rehabilitation at Walter Reed Army Medical Center in Washington, D.C., and Letterman Army Hospital in San Francisco. His assignments took him across the globe, filling positions at Fort Lewis, Washington, as well as in Taiwan and Africa. He also served with the U.S. State Department for a short period. With his outstanding leadership and clinical skills, he succeeded in changing the course of the lives of many severely injured soldiers.

Fred suffered a heart attack while in Africa, which prompted him and his family to decide it was time for him to retire from military service and return to the United States to continue life as a civilian. After recovering, Fred still had a desire to contribute to society in some way, so he worked part-time at juvenile correctional facilities in Orange County, California, providing medical care to youths who found themselves in trouble with the law. He also took a position as a professor with the University of California, Irvine School of Medicine, teaching electromyogram techniques to medical students. Fred and his wife, Kari, retired in Tustin, California. He died on December 8, 2009.

The Lewis brothers continued at the University of Utah, where Bob participated in another NCAA tournament in the spring of 1945—this time in tennis. Shortly afterward they joined the army together, where they both gained entry into a specialized program in electrical engineering. That year only four enlisted men were allowed into the program, and the Lewis twins were half that number. Though they never saw any action on the battlefield, they nevertheless had a chance to serve their country using their wits. After the war they both enrolled at Stanford to continue their engineering studies.

Both Fred and Bob continued pursuing their mutual loves of sports and knowledge at Stanford, and Bob even found a new love there—and married her. Upon graduating from Stanford, the twins began living their lives apart from each other for the first time ever. Bob would spend a few years working in engineering before eventually starting his own venture capital company. All the while he maintained his passion for sports, even managing to beat two U.S. Open tennis champions in different tournaments. Now retired, Bob recently wrote his first book about tennis and spends his time teaching people of all ages the benefits of the sport.

Fred was introduced to his future wife through the basketball coach at Stanford. He worked as an engineer for Hughes Aircraft for most of his career. He was ahead of his time, and used computers for communication in novel ways before the Internet had even been dreamed of. He now volunteers his time in various schools and school districts teaching students and teachers how to utilize technology to learn more efficiently.

As a child who experienced loss and disappointment, Arnie Ferrin could have succumbed to life's challenges. However, his accomplishments with the Utes basketball team as an eighteen-year-old set the course by which he continues to lead his life. His love of sport, family and life in general continues to define his character.

Arnie returned to the University of Utah for the 1944–45 basketball season and led the team to a Skyline Conference Championship and another invitation to the NCAA Tournament. For the second year in a row Arnie was selected as an all-American. However, Uncle Sam had reversed his 4-F draft status, and at the end of conference play he reported for military service. Without Arnie in the lineup, the Utes lost in the first round of the Western Regionals.

He reported to Fort Benning, Georgia, for Officer Candidates School and received a nomination to the U.S. Naval Academy. With the war winding down and the navy needing fewer officers, they offered Arnie the option to continue with his appointment to the academy or return to civilian life. He decided against a military career and returned to the University of Utah in time to play for the Utes during the 1946–47 season. Wat and Dick returned to the university at the same time, and the three returning lettermen gave a boost to Vadal's team, which again won the conference crown and earned a trip all the way to the NIT championship game against Kentucky. This time around the Utes redeemed their 1944 loss to the Wildcats and won the NIT Championship. For the third year in a row Arnie was named an all-American.

During his senior year the team had a record of 17–13 and failed to qualify for postseason play. Nevertheless, Arnie was named as an all-American for the fourth time in his four-year college career, an achievement that has been duplicated by less than a handful of ball-players in all of college basketball history.

Ned Irish, the president of the New York Knickerbockers, called Arnie and asked if he was planning on playing pro ball. If he were, the Knicks were willing to make him their number one pick in the up-coming draft. The life of a professional basketball player wasn't attractive to Arnie at the time, and he felt that he could make more money if he entered the business world. He would also have more time to spend with his wife, RoLayne Rasmussen, the homecoming queen at the University of Utah whom he had married the previous summer, so he declined the offer from the Knicks.

He was selected to play in the college all-star game in Chicago that pitted the best college seniors against the 1948 National Basketball League–champion Minneapolis Lakers. Arnie had a stellar game and was named the Most Valuable Player for the college all-stars. After the game the general manager of the Lakers, which held his draft rights, approached him with an offer. After negotiating for some time that evening, Arnie had a change of heart about a career as a professional basketball player and left the arena as a Laker. He traveled to Minneapolis the next day and reported to the Lakers' office to begin his pro career.

He started at guard for the Lakers for three years. Two of those years the Lakers won their league championship. The fans voted him the most popular player on the team during his second year.

The physical demands of playing the long professional season were immense, and by the end of each season Arnie's six-foot-four-inch frame weighed no more than 140 pounds. He would spend the summer putting on enough weight to begin play the following winter. Being away from his wife and two young children for weeks at a time during the season was taking a toll on Arnie and RoLayne. So instead of signing a contract to play for the Lakers for a fourth season, he decided to retire from pro ball to return to Utah and join his father in business.

After several successful years in business, the call of professional athletics beckoned to him again. In the early 1970s he took a position as general manager of the Utah Stars of the American Basketball Association. One of the highlights of his stint with the Stars was the drafting and signing of a young high school basketball player by the name of Moses Malone, who went on to have a memorable career in the ABA and NBA and is now a member of the Basketball Hall of Fame.

Arnie returned to the University of Utah just before the ABA–NBA merger, accepting the position of director of athletics, a position he held until his retirement in 1989. During his tenure at Utah he served six years on the men's NCAA Basketball Tournament Selection Committee, and in 1988 was elected chairman of the committee. The following year he served as a consultant to CBS in negotiations with the NCAA to purchase the television rights to broadcast NCAA Tournament games. It was the first billion-dollar contract any television network had paid for the rights to televise a sporting event.

In 2003, *Street and Smith's College Basketball* magazine named Arnie one of the best one hundred players in the history of college basketball. In 2005 the University of Utah awarded him an honorary doctorate of humanities for his outstanding service to the university and the community. And in 2008 Arnie was elected to the National Collegiate Basketball Hall of Fame.

Arnie lives in Salt Lake City, five minutes from the university that he has represented most of his life. He attends every home football and basketball game and each gymnastics meet. His retired jersey number 22 hangs from the rafters of the university's Huntsman Center, never to be worn again by another Utah player.

Wat Misaka received his greetings from Uncle Sam the moment he stepped off the train on the team's return from New York in 1944. The army made use of his Japanese heritage and trained him as a translator. He ended up in Japan, interviewing those who had survived the atomic blast at Hiroshima. The first time he stepped onto the soil of his parents' homeland he was there as a foreigner. He was shocked to see that the native Japanese viewed him as working for the enemy. He had spent the first twenty years of his life as an outsider, and now, in the land of his heritage, his own people viewed him as a traitor.

After serving two years in the army he returned to the University of Utah. He expected to play basketball again, but Vadal didn't talk to him, much less ask him to try out for the team. He showed up at practice anyway, only to find his number had been given to a younger player. He made the roster, but wasn't included on the traveling team and again saw little playing time on the court. It wasn't until the 1947 NIT Tournament that Vadal came to his senses and played Wat. In the Utes' return to Madison Square Garden, Wat once more excited the New York crowd as he was pitted with the task of defending Kentucky's top scorer, all-American Ralph Beard. In the '47 NIT final, Wat held the prolific scorer to a single point, which was scored on a free throw off a foul that Wat was sure he didn't commit. Fate replayed itself, and the crowd fell in love with the unlikely basketball hero once again.

Ned Irish, the Garden's basketball director and president of the New York Knickerbockers, saw the uncanny connection Wat had with the New York crowds. So in professional basketball's first draft, the Knicks chose Wat with one of their draft picks, making him the first minority to be drafted and play professional basketball. He beat Chuck Cooper, the first African American ever drafted, by three years.

Wat knew he was up against great odds from the minute he was drafted, but he couldn't pass up the opportunity so he dropped out of college and moved to New York to play for the Knicks. He saw a total of about ten minutes of playing time in three games at the start of the 1947 season, accumulating several steals and a total of seven points. He is one of the shortest players to ever play professional basketball. His teammates treated him as an equal—just as his former teammates had—but the coaching staff may have seen things differently. After his third game, Irish called Wat into his office to let him know he was being cut from the team. There was no explanation; Wat was just told that it was the coaches' decision. He was disappointed and confused, but resilient. Wat couldn't be sure there was any racial motivation, but the question has stayed with him over the years. Over the course of his life he had become used to injustices, and accepted the situation without any bitter feelings. He shed no tears when he left New York.

On his way back to Salt Lake City, Wat received another unlikely invitation while stopping in Chicago. Wat had called his acquaintance, Abe Saperstein, the owner of the Harlem Globetrotters, to catch up. Abe extended Wat an invitation on the spot to play with the Globetrotters, and asked him to hop on a train and join them on the road. Wat politely declined and continued his trip back home.

He returned to the University of Utah and earned his degree in engineering. He eventually ended up at Sperry, a defense contractor in Utah, where he worked on various projects over the years, including one of his favorites: designing rocket engines. Wat is now semiretired and lives in Bountiful, Utah, with his wife of fifty-five years. Both of his children followed in his footsteps and worked with him as engineers.

Wat had an equally illustrious career in bowling. In 1947 he helped found the Japanese American National Bowling Association in Salt Lake City because the American Bowling Congress still had a "white only" clause in its membership requirements. He would later become president of the association and draft its constitution. He is a member of the JANBA Hall of Fame.

In different circumstances, Wat's young life might not have seemed remarkable. Time, place, politics and environment—all aligned at the perfect moment for a talented and humble young man to step up and help change the way America viewed itself. Those who come along at the right time to make a difference for the rest of us rarely realize they are blazing a trail. More often than not they, like Wat, are operating on instinct, doing no more than what they think anyone should do.

Even after all these years Wat is still unsure of why people think so highly of his accomplishments in life. From his perspective, his experiences didn't seem all that monumental as he was living them. He was doing the same thing any young man does: following his dreams and making the most of the opportunities that came his way.

Wat didn't have a goal of challenging people's perceptions of Japanese Americans, of breaking down prejudices—he didn't even consciously bring up the subject of race very often. What he accomplished is remarkable because he was just doing what he wanted to, and he didn't allow others' perceptions to impede his progress.

History has a way of making heroes obsolete. The current overcommercialization of sports has exacerbated the problem by elevating athletes to the status of idols. Trends come and go, passing from today's hot fashion into the annals of history. The early pioneers of basketball have been nearly forgotten in today's world of frenetic marketing and promotion. Those early players had simpler motivations and much less training, but their victories were no less epic in the realization of their vivid childhood dreams—especially for a special group of young kids from Utah. Years after their feats on the basketball court, the reality of what they accomplished still leaves them spellbound.

As a tribute to the Cinderella team of 1944, the University of Utah commissioned a thirty-foot-long bas-relief sculpture that graced one of the interior walls of the Einar Nielson Field House. It depicted a moment during the team's fateful NIT loss to Kentucky: Arnie leaping through the air to intercept a stray pass, and Wat with his hands raised in anticipation in the background. For decades it served as a visual reminder to the students at the school of the amazing accomplishments of a few dedicated and talented student athletes who started at the bottom and made their way to the top of the world.

When the time came to renovate the Field House, the plaster sculpture was carefully removed and placed outside the gym to await its restoration to its place of prominence. A storm appeared, dousing the sculpture with rain for several hours. The plaster homage quickly dissolved under the downpour, creating small, milky streams that ran down the sidewalk away from the gym and into the grass. It has never been replaced and exists today only in the memories of those old enough to remember it.

Like the sculpture, most have forgotten about the miracle of 1944. Utah has not won another championship since 1947. The only two championships in the school's history came in 1944 and 1947—coincidentally the only two years Arnie, Wat and Dick played together. The players wear no championship rings on their fingers—they received watches instead—and their names grace few books. From time to time, whenever a freshman garners enough media attention in the NCAA Tournament, the records are dusted off and commentators recall the spindly blond beanpole from Utah—Arnie Ferrin, the first freshman to be named the tournament's Most Outstanding Player.

Wat's role in the history of basketball, as the first minority ever drafted and the first to play professional basketball, is virtually unknown. But to him and all the other Utah players, prominence or recognition means little. They never set out to win attention or fame, and it was a surprise to them when it happened. They simply had a passion that could not be contained in spite of the seemingly insurmountable obstacles. They are content to have been participants in a victory, both tragic and beautiful, the likes of which we will probably never see again.

ACKNOWLEDGMENTS

It goes without saying that *Blitz Kids* wouldn't be a book without the help of many. As this is our first book, we are delighted and a bit shocked to see years of work finally sitting on a bookshelf. It was not easy, and at times it did not seem likely. But with much help, this book came to be. It is with that thought in mind and with a deep sense of gratitude that we single out the following for their help, advice, kind criticism, encouragement and loving patience.

Thanks to:

Alan, David and Manny for seeing this story with the same vision we did. Here's to seeing it soon on the big screen.

Mikel Vause and MaryAnn Ferrin for wading through early versions of the manuscript and offering their editorial advice.

Our agent, Farley Chase at Scott Waxman Agency, for taking us on as authors and having faith in the story and in our ability as writers, and for his sage advice and encouragement.

Gibbs Smith, Publisher, for taking a chance with *Blitz Kids* and having the foresight to understand that this tale is more than just a basketball story—it is a universal tale that everyone can relate to. And to Bob Cooper, our editor at Gibbs Smith, who has helped us take this great story and make it into a great book.

Lorraine Crouse, photo archivist in the Special Collections Department at the J. Willard Marriott Library, University of Utah, and Kirk Baddley, archivist at the University of Utah Archives, for granting us access to photographs and papers relating to the 1944 Utes.

Anne Prichard, archivist at the University of Arkansas Libraries Special Collections, for contributing documents and articles regarding the 1944 University of Arkansas basketball team.

Weber State University Stewart Library Special Collections for allowing us access to photos of the early careers of both Wat and Arnie.

The *Deseret News* for access to their photo archive.

Joy Peterson, who gave us special insight into Vadal's life and personality.

George Kok and writer Charles Chandler for providing insight into the tale of the University of Arkansas basketball team's tragic story.

RoLayne Ferrin, the matriarch of the Ferrin family. If we claim any writing ability at all, it descends directly through her genes. Her love and influence is still felt strongly many years after her passing. We wish she could be here to see the telling of this story come to be.

The team, the '44 Utes, who lived something most of us can only dream about, and for being champions in life long after their basketball careers ended. Thanks for enduring long hours of questions and interviews with us, telling us your secrets so we could better capture the time and place of your remarkable story. Thank you for living storyworthy lives.

Our families and friends for just being there for us and sharing our enthusiasm.

A special thanks to Tara Ferrin, my wife. I have no shortage of wild ideas, and somehow you have yet to tire of hearing them. Thank you for your patience, your love and your unending support.

To my children, Oliver, who slept on my lap as I wrote this book in the wee hours of the morning; and Lincoln, who listens to this story with as much joy as I did as a child. Thanks for listening to all my stories. May there be many more to come.

To my writing partner and father. Thanks for saying yes when I had the crazy idea to write this book. It would not have happened without you.

—Josh Ferrin

I owe a special debt of gratitude to my wife and life's partner, Sherry Ferrin. Thank you for being patient when being a husband, friend and father took second place to being a writer. Thanks for jumping on board and going for this ride.

Agreeing to write a book with a family member has the potential for a disastrous outcome. With you, Josh, the journey was exceptional.

—Tres Ferrin

INDEX